AF577335

TOUCHDOWN!
Football's Most Dramatic Scoring Feats

TOUCHDOWN!
Football's Most Dramatic Scoring Feats

edited by Phyllis and Zander Hollander

illustrated with photographs

A Zander Hollander Sports Book

Random House New York

Copyright © 1982 by Associated Features Inc.
All rights reserved under International and Pan-American Copyright Conventions.
Published in the United States by Random House, Inc., New York, and simultaneously in Canada by Random House of Canada Limited, Toronto.

Library of Congress Cataloging in Publication Data:
Main entry under title: Touchdown!: football's most dramatic scoring feats.
(Random House sports library) "A Zander Hollander sports book."
Summary: A collection of more than fifty stories about professional and collegiate football players who have made touchdown history.
1. Football—History—Addresses, essays, lectures—Juvenile literature.
2. Football players—Addresses, essays, lectures—Juvenile literature.
[1. Football—History. 2. Football players]
I. Hollander, Phyllis. II. Hollander, Zander. III. Series.
GV954.T68 796.332 82-575
ISBN: 0-394-85020-3 (pbk.); 0-394-95020-8 (lib. bdg.) AACR2

All of the photographs in this book appear courtesy of United Press International with the exception of: Mitchell B. Reibel/Fotosport, page 6; George Gojkovich, page 15; Richard Pilling, page 21; University of Alabama/Sports Photo Source, page x; Brigham Young/Sports Photo Source, page 121; Cornell University/Sports Photo Source, page 98; Detroit Lions/Sports Photo Source, page 2; Houston Oilers/Sports Photo Source, page 38; University of Pittsburgh/Sports Photo Source, page 115; University of Southern California/Sports Photo Source, page 119.

Manufactured in the United States of America
1 2 3 4 5 6 7 8 9 0

Acknowledgments

Out of the huddle came a team of specialists who made *Touchdown!* possible. The editors acknowledge with appreciation the contributions of writers Howard Blatt, Eric Compton, and Frank Kelly; photo researcher Nat Andriani; as well as the college sports information directors and the publicity men of the National Football League.

Contents

38

Introduction

A referee in a white-striped shirt, his arm raised skyward, says it all—Touchdown! His is the signal that brings a roar from the crowd, a groan from the defensive team and its rooters, and the flashing of six points on the scoreboard.

No matter how it comes—on a run, a pass, the return of a kickoff, a blocked kick, a recovered fumble—the touchdown is the most exciting event in football.

In the more than 50 stories that follow, you will meet the professional and college players whose records or unusual feats made touchdown history—often in the closing seconds of the game.

Discover the quarterback who threw the shortest touchdown pass; the ball-carriers who made the longest runs and the most touchdowns; the kick-return specialist who ended the quickest overtime game; and dozens of other players who have had a hand in the legend of the touchdown.

And for instant reference, there is an appendix with all-time touchdown records for the National Football League (including Super Bowls) and the National Collegiate Athletic Association.

—Phyllis and Zander Hollander

TOUCHDOWN!
Football's Most Dramatic Scoring Feats

Billy Sims of the Detroit Lions scored 16 times in his rookie season.

THE ROAR OF A LION

Billy Sims was the number 1 pick in the National Football League (NFL) draft in 1980. Now he was being introduced at Anaheim Stadium in California on the opening day of the 1980 season, his first as a professional. As the nation's top college football player in 1978, this running back from the University of Oklahoma had been awarded the Heisman Trophy.

But on September 7, Sims was only a rookie in the world of the pros. He was starting for the Detroit Lions against the Los Angeles Rams. The Ram fans who came to see their National Football Conference (NFC) champions were not prepared for the difference one running back could make in a Detroit Lion team that had won only two games in 1979.

It was the opening quarter when Sims broke loose, slashed through the Rams' line, and pounded across the goal line from 10 yards out for his first pro touchdown. Before the afternoon was over,

Sims had scored twice more—on a one-yard plunge and a 44-yard gallop—and gained 153 yards in the Lions' 41–20 upset victory.

The three TD's were only chapter one in an incredible first year for Sims. Before the last gun had sounded in 1980, Billy Sims had crossed the goal line 13 more times. His 16 scores represented the highest total of any pro rookie since Gale Sayers had broken in with the Chicago Bears by scoring 22 TD's in 1965. Sims had scored more touchdowns in a single season than any previous Lion, 13 of them on rushes (a club record) and the other three on pass receptions.

Sims's stunning arrival in the pros placed him high in the ranks of rookie running backs who had a nose for the goal line. Buffalo's Cookie Gilchrist pounded his way to 15 TD's in 1962, Dallas' Tony Dorsett wound up with 13 in 1977, and Houston's Earl Campbell raced his way to 13 in 1978.

A VOICE IN THE HUDDLE

The San Francisco 49ers had a problem on September 21, 1980, when they came to Shea Stadium in New York City to play the New York Jets. The 49er quarterback, Steve DeBerg, had a severe case of laryngitis. So the 49ers equipped him with a special amplifier system that fitted under his uniform. At least his signals would be heard.

In the first quarter the 49ers were at the Jets' five-yard line when DeBerg left the game, supposedly to have his amplifier worked on. In came backup quarterback Joe Montana, who had not played at all in the 49ers' first two games. The Jets probably figured Montana would play it safe until DeBerg could return. But on the first play, Montana circled right end and scooted into the end zone for a touchdown.

In the second quarter, with the 49ers leading, 14–0, Montana came in for DeBerg again. The Jets were now wary of Montana's running skills, so the 49er quarterback passed to Dwight Clark for a 20-yard touchdown.

San Francisco's Joe Montana found the range against the New York Jets in 1980.

Montana, a Notre Dame graduate, replaced De-Berg near the Jet goal line again in the third quarter and once more hit Clark, this time for a seven-yard touchdown that put the game out of reach.

The 49ers won, 37–27. Montana threw only six passes, but completed four for 60 yards and two scores.

DeBerg had not only lost his voice, but he lost his job when Montana went on to become the 49ers' starting quarterback. And in 1982 Montana became the Most Valuable Player (MVP) in the Super Bowl after leading San Francisco to victory over Cincinnati.

DOUBLE OVERTIME

Quarterback Ken (The Snake) Stabler has had several outstanding receivers in his career—Fred Biletnikoff, Cliff Branch, Raymond Chester. But his favorite has to be Dave Casper, his tight end at both Oakland and Houston. When Stabler was traded to Houston in 1980, he got off to a slow start and asked the Oilers to make a deal for Casper. They did, and the two combined to lead the team into the playoffs.

Their greatest joint effort, however, was in a playoff game three years earlier, on December 24, 1977, when the Oakland Raiders met the Baltimore Colts in the American Football Conference semifinals at Baltimore's Municipal Stadium.

The lead changed hands eight times, and there were several big plays—Clarence Davis' 30-yard run for Oakland's opening TD, Marshall Johnson's 87-yard kickoff return, and Bruce Laird's 61-yard interception return, the last two for Baltimore touchdowns.

But the biggest play, according to Stabler, didn't result in a touchdown. It came with just over a minute to play in regulation time and the Colts leading, 31–28. Casper made a great over-the-shoulder catch for a 43-yard gain to the Baltimore 14-yard line. Three plays later Errol Mann kicked a 22-yard field goal to send the game into sudden-death overtime. The first team to score would be the winner.

Neither team could score in the first overtime, but as the 15-minute period ended, Stabler was driving the Raiders deep into Baltimore territory. The "sixth quarter" began with the ball on the Colt 13. Pete Banaszak carried the ball to the 10. On that play Raider coach John Madden noticed that "the Colts were playing exclusively for the run . . . so we decided to fake the run and throw to Casper."

It wasn't easy. Casper had to fight off a linebacker before getting clear in the left corner. And Stabler's pass was high, forcing Casper to reach up and out to snare it. But he did, so 43 seconds into the second overtime period, Stabler and Casper had combined for their fourth pass completion of the day—three of them for touchdowns—and Oakland won the sudden-death playoff, 37–31.

The three TD receptions by Casper tied the record for that category in NFL post-season playoffs. But Casper played down his winning catch. "Any stiff could have done it," he said.

As for Stabler, he insisted it wasn't the key play of the game. "We could have kicked a field goal and still won the game. Without Dave's catch in the last minute of regulation play, we might never have played the other scene."

GALE FORCE

The 1965 NFL season was nearing its end when a friend told Gale Sayers, "You've got a shot at becoming Rookie of the Year, but you've got to have a good day against San Francisco." That was all the Chicago Bears' running back had to hear as he prepared for the game on December 12 at Wrigley Field in Chicago.

The All-American from the University of Kansas got off to a fast start. He took a screen pass from Rudy Bukich, then wiggled, squirmed, and dodged through the entire 49er team, taking the pass 80 yards for a score. Late in the second quarter Sayers added a touchdown run of 21 yards. Just before the half, the Bears closed in on the 49er goal and again called on Gale. Result: a seven-yard touchdown, his third of the game.

In the third quarter Sayers took a screen pass 50 yards for a fourth touchdown and then added a fifth score on a one-yard dive. Now he was within one touchdown of the all-time record for TD's in an

NFL game, held by Ernie Nevers and Dub Jones. But with the Bears leading, 40–13, coach George Halas didn't want to take any chances on Sayers getting injured. He decided Gale would not carry the ball from scrimmage again. If he was to tie the record, it would have to be on a kickoff or punt return.

Finally Sayers got his chance. The 49ers were forced to punt from their 43. Sayers went back to the Bears' 15 and waited. Eleven frustrated 49ers, determined to stop him in any way possible, bore down on Sayers. He took the ball and headed straight upfield. Just as the defenders closed in on him, he sidestepped, veering left. Once the defenders made their move that way, Gale broke the other way. No one laid a hand on him as he streaked 85 yards for his sixth touchdown of the day, tying Nevers and Jones.

The touchdown was also Sayers' twenty-second of the season, an all-time record for rookies. And, of course, he received the Rookie of the Year award.

BLOWING HIS HORN

The record book doesn't say how many players in NFL history have played the French horn. One who did, however, was Al Nelson, who performed as a cornerback for the Philadelphia Eagles for nearly a decade, starting in 1965.

Nelson was a college star at the University of Cincinnati, his hometown, and he made the NFL All-Rookie team in his first professional season. The following year, on December 11, 1966, at Philadelphia's Franklin Field, he was on his own goal line defending against a field-goal attempt by the Cleveland Browns. The kick was off target; Nelson grabbed it and ran 100 yards for a touchdown.

It was an NFL record for the longest return of a missed field goal, which Nelson held by himself until Green Bay Packer Ken Ellis raced 100 yards on a missed field-goal attempt by the New York Giants on September 19, 1971, at Green Bay's Lambeau Field.

The 5-foot-11, 186-pound Nelson was not content to share his record. The very next week, on September 26, 1971, at Philadelphia's Veterans Stadium, he was one yard into the end zone in a game against the Dallas Cowboys. Again an attempt at a field goal was unsuccessful, and again he came up with the ball and turned it into a touchdown, this time scampering 101 yards for a new record.

He had every reason to blow his horn.

BROADWAY JOE'S SECRET WEAPON

Everybody knew him as Broadway Joe, the colorful quarterback who had led the New York Jets to victory in Super Bowl III in 1969. But now it was 1974 and times had changed. The Jets' team was being rebuilt with younger players under new coach Charlie Winner, and Namath was reportedly finding it harder and harder to play because of the constant pain in his surgically scarred knees. Still, Joe wouldn't quit.

On November 10 the Jets, who had lost seven of their first eight games, were playing the New York Giants, their archrivals, at Yale Bowl in New Haven, Connecticut. In the fourth quarter the Jets were trailing, 20–13, and time was running short. But Namath drove his team to the Giants' three-yard line and called for a play that would have Emerson Boozer try to run the ball over. However, Namath, after taking the snap, faked the handoff to Boozer and instead put the ball on his hip and hobbled around the right side for the tying touchdown.

Namath had surprised everyone, including his own teammates.

It was his first touchdown in five years, and later Namath would top off his performance by throwing a five-yard TD pass to Boozer in overtime, giving the Jets a 26–20 victory.

Joe Namath of the New York Jets, like all quarterbacks, got opinions on the sideline earphones from the assistant coaches, but he chose his own moves against the New York Giants in 1974.

Namath, of course, was much more famous for his arm, which could fire a ball 60 yards on a line. A native of Beaver Falls, Pennsylvania, Joe played for Bear Bryant at Alabama before signing a $400,000 contract with the Jets. At the time, contracts that large were unheard of.

He quickly developed into one of the game's top quarterbacks, in spite of his bad knees. In 1969 he led the Jets to a stunning Super Bowl win over the Baltimore Colts, a game that is still looked upon as a landmark in pro ball since it gave the upstart American Football League a surprising victory over the established National Football League.

Namath left the Jets after the 1976 season and spent a year with the Los Angeles Rams before retiring. He holds Jet team records for TD passes in a game (six, vs. Baltimore on September 24, 1972) and TD passes in a career (170). Anyone who ever saw him will never forget how he could pass for a score from virtually anywhere on the field.

DO-IT-ALL COLT

When pro football people talk about running backs who can do it all, they mean players who can run, block, and catch passes. Lenny Moore of the Baltimore Colts was just such a player. An explosive runner with great pass-catching instincts, Moore was most dangerous near the end zone.

In a game against the Washington Redskins in 1963, Moore scored on a short TD run. The following week he scored again. And again the next week. In every game of the 1964 season Moore scored at least once. In the 1965 season opener he scored once. Finally, in a loss to Green Bay, Moore's touchdown streak was snapped. He had scored at least one touchdown in 18 straight games, an NFL record.

When he retired following the 1967 season, Moore had scored 113 touchdowns, second behind Jimmy Brown in the record book. He had run for 63 scores, caught 48 TD passes, and had returned two kicks for scores. He had truly done it all.

THE O.J. EXPLOSION

His real name was Orenthal James Simpson, but to the NFL he was just O.J. And he may have been the best running back the game has ever seen. He came out of Southern California as a Heisman Trophy winner and the number 1 draft choice overall, selected by the Buffalo Bills in 1969.

He turned the Bills into contenders in the early 1970s, breaking Jimmy Brown's single-season rushing record by gaining 2,003 yards in 1973. But it was two years later that "The Juice" had perhaps his best season.

Used more as a receiver than ever before, Simpson started to score touchdowns at a record pace. On December 20, going into the final game of 1975 against the Minnesota Vikings at Buffalo's Rich Stadium, O.J. had scored 21 times, only one less than the record for most touchdowns in a season set by Gale Sayers of the Chicago Bears in 1965.

He scored once in the first half to tie Sayers' record, but Minnesota's Chuck Foreman, who was also having a remarkable year, had scored four times, making his total for the year 22 as well. O.J. wanted the record.

With the Vikings leading, 35–7, in the third quarter and the ball on Buffalo's 36-yard line, Simpson suggested a play to Buffalo quarterback Gary Marangi. It called for O.J. to circle out of the backfield and run a sideline pattern. The pass was short, but O.J. gathered it in. He took off down the sideline, shook off two Viking tacklers around midfield, and was gone. Touchdown!

Simpson had his twenty-third score, a record that stands today in spite of the fact that the league has added two games to its regular-season schedule.

Buffalo's O.J. Simpson, on the way to a touchdown against Pittsburgh in 1975, ended up with the record that year.

THE PRIDE OF AUGUSTANA

How does a man from Augustana College make it in the National Football League? He does it with his arm. Quarterback Ken Anderson wasn't highly thought of by the pro scouts when he graduated in 1971 from little Augustana in Illinois.

His college statistics were impressive, but when the scouts saw who Augustana had been playing, many were turned off. The Cincinnati Bengals, though, knew better. They drafted Anderson in the third round in a move that has paid off handsomely.

Anderson took over the Bengals' number 1 job full-time in 1972 and became one of the NFL's leading quarterbacks. In 1973 he threw 18 touchdown passes and guided the Bengals, a franchise only six years old, into the playoffs. Though the team slumped the following season, Anderson was even better, completing 65 percent of his passes and again connecting for 18 scores. In a game against Pittsburgh that year, Anderson set a record for completing passes, hitting 20 out of 22 attempts, or 90.91 percent.

He had perhaps his finest year in 1981, steering the Bengals to the American Football Conference (AFC) Central Division title and leading the NFL in passing. Cincinnati advanced all the way to the Super Bowl, which they lost to the San Francisco 49ers. Fittingly, on the final day of the regular season Anderson threw two TD passes that helped the Bengals pull out a two-point win over the Atlanta Falcons. That gave him a career-high 29 TD passes for the season and a Bengal-record 160 for his career.

Ken Anderson's passes make him the Cincinnati Bengal record-holder.

ONE SUPER SCORE

It was January 18, 1976, and the situation was desperate for the Dallas Cowboys in Super Bowl X in Miami. The Cowboys, who had made it into the playoffs as a wild-card entry, were trailing the Pittsburgh Steelers, 21–10, in the fourth quarter.

Coach Tom Landry decided to go to a three-player wide-receiver offense, and for his third man he chose Percy Howard, a little-known, little-used rookie from Austin Peay in Clarksville, Tennessee. What made the selection surprising was that Howard had not played football in college (he was a basketball star) and had not caught a pass all year for the Cowboys.

Quarterback Roger Staubach brought the Cowboys to the Steelers' 34 and then called a play designed for the rookie. Howard went deep toward the goal line against All-Pro cornerback Mel Blount. At the last second the rookie faked a move and the veteran Blount fell down. Staubach's pass hit Howard in the end zone. Touchdown! The man who had never caught a pass in his professional career had scored a Super Bowl touchdown.

Unfortunately for the Cowboys time ran out and they lost, 21–17, to Pittsburgh. And unfortunately for Howard, he was cut by Dallas the following season. But he had had his moment of glory as the only man in history to turn his one pass reception into a Super Bowl score.

MONSTERS OF THE MIDWAY

Nobody could possibly have been prepared for what happened at Griffith Stadium in Washington, D.C., on December 8, 1940.

The Washington Redskins were playing the Chicago Bears for the NFL championship. The Redskins had beaten the Bears, 7–3, earlier in the year.

Everybody expected the game to be a close duel between Washington's great passing game—featuring quarterback Sammy Baugh and receivers Frank Filchock and Roy Zimmerman—and the strong Chicago ground game. The Bears of that era had as their backbone a huge line to open holes for breakaway backs like George McAfee, Bullet Bill Osmanski, Ray Nolting, and Joe Maniaci.

The Chicago team had an outstanding passer in Sid Luckman, but they were not primarily a passing team, and on this Sunday they would hardly throw at all.

During the week before the game, the Bears had been forced to practice indoors because there was a foot of snow in Chicago. After the train ride to Washington they couldn't wait to practice outdoors in snowless Griffith Stadium.

Washington's Andy Farkas, a running back, remembered how the Bears looked coming out on the field the day before the game. "They were screaming like a pack of Indians. I'd never seen anything like it. They took off and ran the length of the field. They circled the goal posts and started back, and they were still screaming."

Their enthusiasm carried over into the game itself. On the third play Osmanski took a pitchout from Luckman and went around left end for 68 yards and a touchdown. The Redskins struck back quickly, moving down to the Bears' 19, but were unable to score as they missed on a field-goal attempt. The Bears then marched 81 yards to a touchdown without throwing a single pass, Luckman going over on a one-foot sneak.

Before the first period ended, the Bears had scored again on a run by Maniaci. In the second quarter Luckman's pass to Ken Kavanaugh produced another touchdown.

As the game developed it was clear that Luckman didn't have to throw. His running mates were tearing off long runs for touchdowns almost at will. In the third period the Bears picked up four more touchdowns, three on intercepted passes. They got three more in the fourth quarter, two by Harry Clark, a substitute.

The reeling Redskins never got to score a point!

The Bears ended up with 11 touchdowns. When the final gun sounded, the score was Chicago 73, Washington 0.

It was the most lopsided game in NFL history, and from then on the Bears from the Middle West were called the Monsters of the Midway.

THE GIFFER

Former football players often turn to broadcasting after their playing days are over. Some make it; some don't. One who successfully made the change is Frank Gifford, the ABC-TV commentator known as the Giffer on *Monday Night Football.*

He was a treat to watch as a football player, starting in the days when he was a triple-threat tailback at Bakersfield Junior College in California. This son of an oil-field worker didn't stop there. He went on to All-America honors as a backfield star at the University of Southern California and to selection as the New York Giants' top draft choice in 1952.

He carried the ball for a mere 101 yards in his first season, and he thought his only chance to stay on the team was to play defense. For a couple of years that was his main assignment. In the mid-1950s, though, he was back on offense, performing in a starring role that brought him NFL Most Valuable Player honors in 1956, the year he led the Giants to the championship.

But on November 20, 1960, Gifford's career seemed to be over. That was the day he was knocked unconscious by a jarring tackle from Chuck Bednarik of the Philadelphia Eagles. The injury forced him to retire from pro football.

In 1961 he scouted for the Giants and did a sports show for CBS. But he couldn't stay away from football, and in 1962 he made a comeback—at a new position, flanker back. There he had a chance to contribute as a pass-catcher. He proved he hadn't lost any of the abilities that had made him All-Pro, and he was voted Comeback Player of the Year as the Giants won the Eastern Division championship.

When he retired again after the 1964 season, Gifford had scored 78 touchdowns, a Giant career record that has never been broken.

The New York Giants' Frank Gifford runs for daylight against Philadelphia in 1963.

TARGET FOR A DAY

When Japanese bombs fell on Pearl Harbor on December 7, 1941, and America was suddenly plunged into World War II, Bob Shaw had just finished his sophomore season as an end on the Ohio State football team.

He was a big guy—6-foot-4, 220 pounds—with ideal dimensions for a football receiver, or for a basketball player. He did go on to play basketball that winter for the Buckeyes. In the fall he returned to football for a junior season in which his pass-catching helped the team win the Big Ten and the national championship in 1942.

Because he was drafted, Shaw never got to play again at Ohio State, but after the hostilities had ended, he became a professional football player. And on October 2, 1950, at Chicago's Comiskey Park, he was an offensive end playing for the Chicago Cardinals against the Baltimore Colts.

The Cardinal quarterback was Jim Hardy, and he found a perfect target in Bob Shaw. Five times he threw touchdown passes to Shaw—and another one to Fran Polsfoot. It added up to a 55–13 victory for the Cardinals.

More than that, Shaw's five TD receptions added up to an NFL record for most TD passes caught in a game. It was tied by Kellen Winslow of San Diego against Oakland on November 22, 1981.

RETURN OF THE CENTURY

The kickoff by Dallas Cowboy Rafael Septien was long and true, sailing well into the St. Louis Cardinals' end zone. Rookie Roy Green, who came out of little Henderson State University in Arkansas, caught the ball and started downfield at Texas Stadium.

One by one the Cowboy defenders made their moves on Green. But the Cardinals made some key blocks and suddenly there was daylight. Green shot for it and in an instant he was out of reach, heading into the end zone. It was the most electrifying moment possible in a football game—the return of a kickoff from end zone to end zone for a touchdown.

It happened on October 21, 1979. Green had traveled, according to the public address announcement, 108 yards, an NFL record—two yards longer than the mark set by the Green Bay Packers' Al Carmichael against the Chicago Bears on October 7, 1956, and tied by Noland Smith of the Kansas

City Chiefs against the Denver Broncos on December 17, 1967.

A couple of days later Cowboy coaches were studying the game films when Green's run came up on the screen. It was then that they realized that Green hadn't gone 108 yards. The films showed Green's position when he received the ball. He was straddling the top of one of the letters that spell out "Texas Stadium" on the turf. A club official measured from that spot to the goal line and found it was six yards, not eight. Instead of setting the record, the rookie defensive back had tied the mark of Carmichael and Smith.

Still, 106 yards was no small feat.

LITTLEST PASS

He was known as the Little General because he was a tiny quarterback—5-foot-7, weighing 167 pounds. Eddie LeBaron had earned his nickname during his seven years with the Washington Redskins. But on October 9, 1960, he was the quarterback of the Dallas Cowboys, and he was playing against his old team at Griffith Stadium in Washington.

The Cowboys were losing, 19–7, in the middle of the fourth quarter, and Eddie drove his team downfield to the Washington one-yard line. On the next two plays he gave the ball to fullback Don McIlhenny, who moved it to within two inches of the goal line. It was third down.

The Washington defenders were expecting another play through the middle. But the Little General surprised them. He stepped back and threw a short pass to Dick Bielski. Touchdown!

Washington went on to win the game, 26–14, but LeBaron had made the record book with what is officially the shortest scoring pass ever thrown in the National Football League—a two-incher.

WRONG-WAY MARSHALL

Like most defensive ends, Jim Marshall rarely made newspaper headlines. But he played for 19 seasons with the Minnesota Vikings, beginning in 1961. He started every regular-season and post-season game for those 19 years, adding up to an NFL record of 280 in a row.

He will be known more, however, for one game he played in 1964 that will always haunt him.

The Vikings were playing the San Francisco 49ers in San Francisco on October 24. Minnesota was leading, 20–17, in the fourth quarter. George Mira, the 49er quarterback, was hit so hard by Marshall that the ball popped loose. Carl Eller, the Vikings' other defensive end, scooped up the ball and rambled 45 yards for a touchdown, putting Minnesota ahead, 27–17.

Following the kickoff, Mira had the 49er offense on the move. He threw a pass to Billy Kilmer, who caught it but fumbled. Marshall, whose coach, Norm Van Brocklin, had called him "the fastest ani-

Minnesota's Jim Marshall picks up the fumble, runs with it, and is then congratulated by San Francisco's Bruce Bosley!

mal I have ever seen on a pro football line," picked up the loose ball and headed for the goal line—the Minnesota goal line—66 yards away.

The roar of the crowd drowned out his teammates' shouts. Marshall ran into the end zone without opposition. He triumphantly flung the ball into the air. But suddenly he realized something was wrong when San Francisco's Bruce Bosley threw his arms around him and thanked him. Then Viking quarterback Fran Tarkenton ran up and said, "Jim, you went the wrong way, the wrong way."

Jubilant San Francisco fans cheered as two points were added to the 49er score. Instead of scoring a touchdown for Minnesota, Marshall had scored a safety for San Francisco. Minnesota now led, 27–19.

Coach Van Brocklin, who normally had an explosive temper, was surprisingly calm, perhaps because he appreciated the humor of it all. "Forget about it, Jim," he said. "Go back in there and make the fans forget."

Marshall and his teammates were able to have the last laugh. San Francisco picked up three more points on a field goal, but Minnesota won the game, 27–22.

Marshall received thousands of sympathetic letters, one of them from a man named Roy Riegels. In the Rose Bowl on New Year's Day, 1929, Riegels, a roving center for the University of California, had recovered a fumble against Georgia Tech and run 64 yards in the wrong direction. But a teammate caught and tackled Riegels on the one-yard line. Moments later Tech scored on a safety and won the game, 8–7.

From then on he was known as Wrong-Way Riegels, and who better than he could tell Marshall to laugh at his own mistake?

THE EARL OF HOUSTON

The Houston Oilers' Earl Campbell had a reputation as a punishing runner. The 5-foot-11 and 224 pounder, the 1977 Heisman Trophy winner from the University of Texas, was fond of running over tacklers instead of around them. But rarely did he dish out as much punishment to an opponent as he did on November 20, 1978, against the Miami Dolphins at the Astrodome in Houston.

Despite two first-half touchdowns by Campbell, the Oilers seemed headed for defeat. Their quarterback, Dan Pastorini, was tackled for a safety that gave the Dolphins a 23–21 lead with 12 minutes to play.

Eighty yards away from the touchdown that would put them ahead, Houston began its drive. Twice Campbell broke loose for crucial third-down yardage to keep the march alive. He capped it by starting inside and then taking the play outside for 12 yards and his third touchdown, making it Houston 28, Miami 23.

After an interception returned the ball to Hous-

Houston's Earl Campbell rolled for 19 touchdowns in 1979.

ton, Campbell's runs ate away at the time remaining. Then Campbell provided the topper—an 81-yard touchdown sweep around right end, leaving Miami safety Tim Foley groping at his heels behind the line of scrimmage. The run gave Campbell 199 yards on 28 carries for the game. The rookie's four rushing touchdowns broke the Houston team record.

"Earl won't listen to instructions," said his delighted coach, Bum Phillips. "I told him just to get the first down and run out the clock."

The following season Campbell tied the NFL record for rushing touchdowns in a season (19). He shares that honor with Green Bay's Jimmy Taylor and San Diego's Chuck Muncie.

PAYING FOR ONE'S MISTAKES

It is bad enough to fumble away a ball in a crucial situation, but imagine the feeling when the fumble is returned for a score.

The Green Bay Packers' MacArthur Lane must have had that feeling on September 24, 1972, in a game against the Oakland Raiders at Green Bay. Lane fumbled a pitchout near the Oakland goal line, and the ball bounced into the end zone. Instead of falling on the ball for a touchback, Oakland's Jack Tatum picked it up on the dead run and took off down the sideline, not stopping until he crossed the Packer goal line 104 yards away. Tatum's run erased a record 98-yard fumble return by the Bears' George Halas in 1923.

Denver's Bill Thompson, who obviously had a nose for such things, recovered a record four fumbles for touchdowns in his career.

The longest return of an interception is 102 yards, and that record is shared by four players. Bob Smith of Detroit was the first to do it, against Chicago on November 24, 1949. The Giants' Erich Barnes did it against Dallas on October 15, 1961; Kansas City's Gary Barbaro matched it against Seattle on December 11, 1977; and so did Cincinnati's Louis Breeden against San Diego on November 8, 1981.

Ken Houston, who played for Houston and Washington, holds the record for interceptions returned for touchdowns—he did it nine times.

•

THE ODD COUPLE

By the time they had reached the end of their careers, neither one looked like an athlete. Y.A. Tittle was bald and scrawny and his legs were like pencils. George Blanda had strong legs but a pot belly, and his hair had long since turned gray.

But Tittle and Blanda are not linked by their physical appearance; they share a line in the NFL record book. It's right there, under the heading "Most Touchdown Passes, Season." The record is 36, set by Blanda in 1961 and equaled by Tittle in 1963.

Blanda set the record with the Houston Oilers of the upstart American Football League (AFL) and thus never got the credit Tittle received. Y.A. tossed his TD passes for the New York Giants of the NFL.

Unfortunately for Tittle, 1963 was his last hurrah. He was hurt in the championship game against the Chicago Bears that year and was never the same afterward. He retired in 1964.

Blanda, who also shares with Tittle and three others the record for TD passes in a game (7), played through the 1975 season with the Oakland Raiders after leaving the Oilers in 1967.

In a 1968 game Blanda, then 41 years old, had a remarkable afternoon for the Raiders. He threw four touchdown passes, including a 94-yarder, in a 43–7 rout of Denver. He was still winning games for Oakland in the early 1970s, mainly as a place-kicker.

LAST-SECOND MAN

Playing college ball at Tulsa University, Drew Pearson did not get the attention of a receiver from, say, Notre Dame or Southern California. So Pearson went unclaimed in the 1973 college draft.

But the Dallas Cowboys signed him as a free agent. They've never regretted it. Ever since his rookie year, Pearson has made a habit of coming through for the Cowboys in the closing seconds of a game. In the 1973 playoffs he caught an 83-yard TD pass late in the fourth quarter to knock the Los Angeles Rams out of post-season play; the following year he caught a pass in the final seconds to complete a 50-yard TD and give Dallas a crucial win over Washington.

In 1975 Pearson made the most famous catch of his career, grabbing Roger Staubach's pass in the final 20 seconds to eliminate the Vikings from the playoffs.

But Pearson's best overall performance took place in the 1980 playoffs at Atlanta on January 4,

1981. The Cowboys were trailing the Atlanta Falcons, 27–17, with seven minutes left. Quarterback Danny White hit Pearson for 15, then 24, and finally 14 yards for a score, bringing the Cowboys back within a field goal at 27–24. The Dallas defense stopped the Falcons, and the Cowboys got the ball back with 1:48 left.

Then White hit three passes to drive the Cowboys to the Atlanta 23, but time was running out. Finally Pearson broke loose on his pattern and ran clear at the goal line. White laid the ball out to him and Drew gathered it in for a score with 42 seconds to go. It gave the Cowboys another incredible come-from-behind win, 30–27.

For Pearson it was just another case of last-second lightning.

A SUB'S SHINING MOMENT

It usually happens in Hollywood, or on Broadway. The star gets sick, the understudy fills in, and suddenly a new star is born.

But this was a football game in Seattle's Kingdome—between the Seahawks and the New York Jets on December 6, 1981. Jim Zorn, Seattle's starting quarterback, was out of action with a broken leg. The Seahawks, with no proven backup quarterback, were forced to call on untried David Krieg against a fearsome Jet defense.

All week long the fans had wondered just who David Krieg was. Had he actually played college ball at Milton College? Where was Milton College? How can a graduate of a school with 500 students expect to survive in a league full of toughened veterans?

Krieg supplied all the answers. The Seahawks got the ball early, and the young quarterback immediately found Sam McCullum in the end zone for a touchdown. After the teams took turns making touchdowns, the Jets rallied to take a 16–13 lead in the third quarter. But Krieg struck again, this time scoring himself on a one-yard run as the Seahawks pulled ahead again, 20–16.

But the Jets weren't finished. A team hoping to make the playoffs, the New Yorkers came back once more to take a 23–20 lead with nine minutes left. It didn't take Krieg long to pull another rabbit out of his helmet. He drove the Seahawks 77 yards in two plays, the second a 57-yard bomb to receiver Steve Largent behind the Jet secondary. The score wrapped up Seattle's astounding 27–23 win over the Jets.

Krieg finished with impressive statistics: 20 completions in 26 attempts for 264 yards and two touchdowns. He indeed had played at tiny Milton College in Wisconsin. And on a Sunday afternoon in 1981 he'd put it on the map.

A STEELER'S STING

Terry Bradshaw was no stranger to Super Bowl pressure when he led the Pittsburgh Steelers onto the field in Super Bowl XIII on January 21, 1979, in Miami. The blond quarterback from Louisiana Tech had guided the Steelers to titles in 1975 and 1976, throwing a total of three touchdown passes in the victories over the Minnesota Vikings (16–6) and the Dallas Cowboys (21–17).

Now Bradshaw and the Steelers were facing the NFC champion Cowboys again in what was being advertised as the most exciting Super Bowl ever. The game more than lived up to its billing.

Bradshaw got the Steelers on the scoreboard early, throwing a 28-yard touchdown pass to John Stallworth in the first quarter. The Cowboys rallied to take a 14–7 lead in the second quarter, but Bradshaw brought the Steelers back. He hit Stallworth again for a 75-yard touchdown and then, just before halftime, he connected with Rocky Bleier for a seven-yard score that gave Pittsburgh the lead.

Midway through the final quarter he took advantage of a Dallas error to fire an 18-yard TD pass to Lynn Swann. Bradshaw's fourth touchdown pass of the day—a Super Bowl one-game record—added the winning margin as the Steelers held on for a 35–31 victory and their third Super Bowl crown.

A year later Bradshaw threw two more TD passes, giving him a record nine overall in Super Bowls. The Steelers also became the first team ever to win four Super Bowls with a 31–19 decision over the Los Angeles Rams.

Pittsburgh's Terry Bradshaw is about to heave a touchdown pass to Rocky Bleier (20) against Dallas in Super Bowl XIII.

A SUPER BOWL FIRST

It was the night before the first Super Bowl. The Green Bay Packers, champions of the NFL, were set to play the Kansas City Chiefs, champions of the AFL, on January 15, 1967. At last, fans of both leagues would have their showdown.

It was an exciting time in Los Angeles—the Super Bowl would be played in the city's Memorial Coliseum—and around the country as the football world prepared to watch the big match on television.

One Packer who was probably blind to the excitement was Max McGee. At age 34, wide-receiver McGee had little hope that coach Vince Lombardi would use him against the Chiefs. McGee planned to retire after the season.

But when Green Bay's Boyd Dowler left the game with a shoulder injury in the first quarter, McGee was sent in. His first test came when the Packers had the ball on the Chiefs' 37. McGee went deep for a pass, and Bart Starr threw the ball high

Green Bay's Max McGee snares an aerial in the end zone from Bart Starr for a touchdown against Kansas City in Super Bowl I.

toward the goal line. McGee and Chief defensive back Willie Mitchell went up for the ball; only Max came down with it. McGee had scored the first touchdown in Super Bowl history!

Later, in the third quarter, McGee struck again. With the Packers leading, 21–10, Starr sent McGee down the middle. This time the veteran ran past

Mitchell. Starr's pass hit McGee's hands as he cut under the goal posts. Max juggled the ball but held on for the fourth Green Bay touchdown.

It was the score that broke the game wide open and sent the Packers on to a 35–10 victory. Quarterback Starr was voted the Most Valuable Player, but the game, and the day, belonged to an aging receiver who hadn't even been sure he would get to play.

MAN WITH A GOLDEN ARM

He didn't come out of college with a big contract and a new car. In fact, he had to play a year of semi-pro football before the pros would consider him seriously. But a lot of teams wound up kicking themselves because they hadn't realized that Johnny Unitas would one day be one of the game's greatest quarterbacks.

A native of Pittsburgh, he played college ball at the University of Louisville. He was certainly no powerhouse but did well enough to be offered a contract by the Pittsburgh Steelers in the summer of 1955. The Steelers took a look and immediately gave the youngster fare for the bus ride home. He wasn't good enough, they told him.

So Unitas played a year of semi-pro ball and then tried out for the Baltimore Colts in 1956. The rest is history. Taking over as the Colts' starting quarterback in 1957, Unitas became an all-star, throwing for 24 touchdowns. He threw for at least one score in every game that season. He did the same in 1958.

And in 1959. Finally, when the streak was stopped in 1960, Unitas had thrown at least one touchdown pass in 47 straight games, an NFL record.

Before he wound down his career in 1973 with the San Diego Chargers, Unitas had tied the record (4) for leading the NFL the most seasons in touchdown passes, and had fired for 290 scores, a record at the time and second now only to Fran Tarkenton's 342.

He had come a long way from the semi-pros in Pittsburgh to the Pro Football Hall of Fame.

THE ALABAMA ANTELOPE

Three musts for a pass receiver are speed, smart moves, and good hands. And perhaps no one in the history of the NFL combined all three talents better than the Green Bay Packers' Don Hutson.

As a boy growing up in Pine Bluff, Arkansas, Hutson was more known for his collection of pet rattlesnakes than he was for football. His admirers said that Hutson learned some of his slippery moves from watching his snakes.

Nicknamed the Alabama Antelope from his football days at the University of Alabama, Hutson played at a time when ends could measure and weigh, as he did, only 6-foot-1 and 180 pounds. He began his pro career in 1935 and played 11 seasons. He was a master at fooling the opposition. "Hutson is the only man I ever saw who could feint in three directions at the same time," said Greasy Neale, coach of the Philadelphia Eagles.

By the time he hung up his uniform for good, following the 1945 season, the Packer receiver had scored 99 touchdowns on pass receptions, a record that has never been approached. He also shares the record for most touchdown catches in a season (17) with Elroy (Crazylegs) Hirsch of Los Angeles and Bill Groman of Houston.

BRINGING THEM BACK

One of the most important rules of football is, "Don't catch a punt inside your own 10-yard line." The reason for this is that a punt that close to the line will in most cases roll into the end zone for a touchback, bringing the ball out to the 20.

But there are exceptions to the rule, and these exceptions happen when the receiving team has men like Dallas Cowboy Dennis Morgan or Denver Bronco Rick Upchurch to field the punt.

Morgan, who had a short NFL career, made his way into the record book on October 13, 1974, in a game at St. Louis. The Cardinals' Hal Roberts booted a long punt toward the Dallas goal line and Morgan went back to get it. Picking up the ball on his two-yard line, Morgan wove his way through the first group of tacklers and then sped down the sideline. He avoided the final tackler at his own 40-yard line, and the rest of the trip was clear sailing. A 98-yard punt return!

Morgan's run didn't help Dallas win the game

(the Cards triumphed, 31–28) but it did put him up there with Cincinnati's Gil LeFebvre and Minnesota's Charlie West, who also ran back punts 98 yards. LeFebvre was the first 98-yard man, returning a Brooklyn Dodger punt for a touchdown on December 3, 1933. West tied LeFebvre's mark with his run against Washington on November 3, 1968.

Although Denver's Upchurch never returned a punt 98 yards, he was the NFL's most effective punt-return man in the 1970s. Upchurch, the league's all-time leader in punt-return yardage, had an unforgettable afternoon against Cleveland on September 26, 1976. He returned a punt 73 yards for a touchdown early in the game and later ran another one back 47 yards for a second score. Upchurch's two TD's tied a record set (twice) by Detroit's Jack Christiansen and equaled by Dick Christy of the old New York Titans.

Christiansen holds the record for most punts returned for touchdown (8); Upchurch ranks second (6).

SUDDEN DEATH

It has been called by many the greatest game ever played and the turning point of professional football. It was the 1958 NFL championship match between the New York Giants and the Baltimore Colts.

Played on December 28 in Yankee Stadium, New York, it was watched by a sellout crowd and a national television audience of forty million. They saw the Giants' Charlie Conerly and Baltimore's Johnny Unitas match forward passes, with neither team able to get a real edge. Late in the final period Frank Gifford raced 15 yards with a Conerly pass to send New York ahead, 17–14.

But the Colts weren't giving up. Led by quarterback Unitas, they took the ball at their own 14-yard line and began a drive downfield. Unitas connected with Lenny Moore for a key first down and then hit receiver Raymond Berry with three straight passes, bringing the Colts deep into New York territory. With time running out, Baltimore kicker Steve

Myhra booted a 20-yard field goal, tying the score and setting up the NFL's first overtime game. The first team to score would win.

The Giants won the coin toss, received the opening kickoff, and had to punt after missing a first down by a yard. The Colts took over on their 20, and Unitas went back to work. Alternating passes to Berry with runs by Alan Ameche, Unitas moved the Colts back into Giant territory.

He connected with Berry again, bringing the ball to the Giant eight-yard line, easy range for a field goal. Unitas threw to tight end Jim Mutscheller on the one, setting up the next play. It was a simple

Baltimore's Alan Ameche hugs the ball after reaching pay dirt in overtime against the New York Giants.

handoff to Ameche, who plowed over the right side of the Giants' line into the end zone. After eight minutes and fifteen seconds the Baltimore Colts had won in sudden death, 23–17, and were champions of the NFL.

Such a stirring finish, before so wide an audience, would have a major impact on the growing pro game as more and more people began to watch the sport.

ONE-MAN SHOW

It was Thanksgiving Day, 1929, and Ernie Nevers broiled a steak for breakfast in his Chicago apartment. The traditional turkey dinner would come later—after the football game between the Chicago Cardinals and the Chicago Bears.

Ernie was the coach and fullback for the Cardinals, and the game was for the city championship of Chicago. It was a day so cold, only 8,000 shivering spectators were in the stands.

But Nevers warmed up fast, scoring a touchdown on a 10-yard off-tackle run early in the first quarter and another on a five-yard plunge before the period ended. He also placekicked the extra point.

There was nothing that Nevers didn't do. He called the plays, he punted, he placekicked. He added another touchdown and an extra point to give the Cardinals a 20–0 halftime lead.

The Bears came back with a touchdown, but Nevers matched it with a one-yard smash and an extra point in the third period.

The crowd, knowing that Ernie had scored all 27 Cardinal points, began chanting, "Give the ball to Nevers." And Ernie responded by scoring two more touchdowns and an extra point, making the final score, as one sportswriter put it: Nevers 40, Bears 6.

Nobody has ever scored as many points in an NFL game.

THE MIGHTIEST BROWN

"The greatest runner in football history" is what his coach, Paul Brown, called Jimmy Brown in the late 1950s and early 1960s when Jimmy was tearing up the turf for the Cleveland Browns. Jimmy Brown was a dominating runner, combining speed with awesome power and stamina.

He played college ball at Syracuse and was virtually a one-man gang. In his final college game against Colgate on November 17, 1956, he scored six touchdowns and kicked seven extra points for a total of 43 points in Syracuse's 61–7 win. He was drafted by the Browns, and his talents again became evident early in his NFL career.

The 6-foot-2, 225-pound fullback had perhaps his finest day as a pro on November 1, 1959, when the Browns took on the defending champion Baltimore Colts at Baltimore's Municipal Stadium. Early in the second quarter Brown snapped a 3–3 tie when he took a pitchout from Milt Plum and rambled 70 yards for a touchdown. The Colts came back to tie

Cleveland's Jimmy Brown scores one of his 126 touchdowns, against Philadelphia.

it, 10–10, but just before halftime Jimmy ran 17 yards for a second TD to restore the Browns' lead.

The game became a battle between Brown and Baltimore's Johnny Unitas, who also was having a remarkable day. Jimmy scored on a three-yard run, but Unitas' second TD pass cut Cleveland's lead to 24–17. Brown scored for the fourth time on a one-yard plunge only to have Unitas toss another TD pass. Finally Jimmy plunged one yard for another touchdown, his fifth, and the Browns held on for a 38–31 win. Jimmy had rushed for all but 19 of his team's 197 yards and scored all of its touchdowns.

Brown spent only nine years in the NFL, retiring in his prime at the age of 30. In his short career he scored 126 touchdowns, by far the most in the history of the league. He also rushed for a record 12,312 yards and led the league in rushing eight times.

He quit the game in 1966 and went into acting. He has since been in a number of movies, including *The Dirty Dozen* and *100 Rifles.*

FRAN THE SCRAM

He didn't look like a pro quarterback. He wasn't especially tall, he didn't have a rifle arm, and he didn't have a quick release. And he liked running with the ball instead of staying in the safety of the pocket.

From the beginning of his NFL career as a Minnesota Viking in 1961, Fran Tarkenton defied custom and risked injury by his constant running. Defensive tackles can hurt a quarterback, especially one who weighs only 185 pounds.

But Tarkenton suffered only one serious injury in his 18-year career, a broken leg, and that didn't come until his seventeenth season. By that time he had established himself as one of football's all-time quarterbacks.

Frustrating the defense with his mad scrambles for yardage, Tarkenton was known as Fran the Scram. He played 13 years with the Minnesota Vikings, bringing them to the Super Bowl three times, and five years with the New York Giants.

Tarkenton retired while he was still at the top of his game and held several NFL records. In his final season, as a Viking in 1978, he passed for 25 touchdowns. It was the sixth time he had gone over the 20-TD mark. He finished his career with 342 touchdown passes, 52 more than anyone had ever thrown. He'd gained the most yards in passing, 47,003, and had the most passes completed, 3,686.

This multitalented Georgian brought an amazing set of statistics and the savvy of a scrambler into the broadcast booth when he signed a long-term commentator's contract with ABC Sports in 1979.

Minnesota's Fran Tarkenton scrambles against Dallas.

ALMOST 100

Pot-bellied Sonny Jurgensen had always been considered one of the NFL's best passers, but he had the bad luck to play on below-average teams, first with the Philadelphia Eagles and later with the Washington Redskins.

In 1967 the Redskins had an unimpressive record of five wins, five losses, and three ties going into the final game against the New Orleans Saints. Here was a chance for the Redskins to have their first winning season in 12 years. Sonny passed the Saints dizzy, putting the ball up 49 times and completing 26 of his passes. Even so, Washington lost, 30–14.

And on September 15, 1968, the opening day of the next season, after he had undergone elbow surgery, Jurgensen threw his way into the record book in a game against the Chicago Bears.

He tossed four touchdown passes to lead Washington to a 38–28 victory. Other quarterbacks have thrown four touchdown passes in a game, but it was the play he made in the second quarter that left the

Sonny Jurgensen's 99-yarder put the Washington quarterback into rare company.

opposition gasping. The Redskins had the ball on their own one-yard line. Jurgensen, standing deep in his own end zone, rifled a pass to Jerry Allen, who was on the 31-yard line. Allen hauled it in and raced the remaining distance for a touchdown. It was a 99-yard pass-and-run play, equaling the longest ever made in the NFL.

Three other pass-run touchdown combinations who clicked for 99 yards were Frank Filchock to Andy Farkas of the Washington Redskins, vs. the Pittsburgh Steelers on October 15, 1939; George Izo to Bobby Mitchell of the Washington Redskins, vs. the Cleveland Browns on September 15, 1963; and Karl Sweetan to Pat Studstill of the Detroit Lions, vs. the Baltimore Colts on October 16, 1966.

IMMACULATE RECEPTION

If there is one play that stands out among all the plays in the history of the National Football League, it is probably the one that took place in an AFC playoff game in Pittsburgh on December 23, 1972. It brought Christmas to the Steel City two days early.

The Steelers were battling the Oakland Raiders in the final minutes and seemingly needed a miracle to win. Ken Stabler had run 30 yards for a score, and George Blanda's extra point had given Oakland a 7–6 lead. There were 73 seconds left.

Terry Bradshaw threw two passes to move the Steelers from their 20 to their 40, but three incomplete passes in a row put the Steelers in a do-or-die situation, fourth-and-10 from the 40, with 22 seconds to play. Bradshaw called for a short pass to Preston Pearson, with Franco Harris staying in the backfield to block.

But the play broke down when the Raiders pressured Bradshaw, and Harris instinctively took off downfield. Bradshaw never saw him, and instead fired the ball toward John Fuqua at the Oakland 35. But just as Fuqua reached for the pass, he bumped into Raider defender Jack Tatum. The ball bounced off the players—toward Harris.

He scooped the ball up at knee level and headed downfield. He raced down the sideline and went into the end zone untouched as the crowd in Three Rivers Stadium went wild.

The officials, however, did not signal a touchdown. If Fuqua alone had deflected the ball, then the play was illegal. If both Tatum and Fuqua had deflected it, it was a touchdown. The referees, after viewing the replay on television, made their decision: Touchdown!

The Steelers had won, 13–7, on a play that would be referred to forever as the "Immaculate Reception."

While that score is the most famous of the many Harris made, the Steelers' running back went on to a brilliant career—especially in clutch situations. He holds the career record for Super Bowl touchdowns (4).

THE ICE BOWL

There were the Green Bay Packers, stuck on the Dallas Cowboys' one-yard line with the clock running out.

It was a cold New Year's Eve, 1967, in Green Bay, and a crowd of 50,000 were frozen in their seats—from excitement and from the 13-below-zero temperature. The Cowboys led, 17–14, and had stopped Green Bay on two previous downs from the one-yard line. The Packers had no time-outs left, so it had all come down to one play.

Quarterback Bart Starr didn't want to risk another handoff because of the cold, so he suggested to coach Vince Lombardi that they try a quarterback sneak through a hole that would have to be made by guard Jerry Kramer. Starr went back to the huddle and called the play while Kramer ground his spikes into the frozen field, trying for better traction.

Starr took the snap, and Kramer drove his shoulder into the Cowboys' Jethro Pugh, sending the tackle a foot into the end zone. The block gave Starr just enough of a hole and he fell forward.

Kramer never saw the referee signal touchdown, but he didn't have to. The roar of the frozen faithful in the stands was all he needed to hear. Starr had scored, and the Packers had won the NFL title, 21–17.

Lombardi could have taken the easy way out and ordered a field-goal attempt from short range, which would have tied the score and sent the game into overtime. But as the Green Bay coach said in the closing minutes, "If we can't get the ball into the end zone in three plays from the one-yard line, we don't deserve to be champions."

The Packers had proved they deserved it.

OPENING GUN

Professional football teams go to training camp in July, working out the kinks of the off-season and practicing hard so they'll be ready for the opening game in the first week of September. Every coach wants his team to get off to a good start, ideally from the opening kickoff.

This was especially so with Ray Malavasi, coach of the Los Angeles Rams on September 7, 1980, when the Detroit Lions came to town. The Rams had made it to the Super Bowl in January, only to lose to the Pittsburgh Steelers.

Now they were raring to go once more. The Rams won the coin toss, and Malavasi sent receiver Drew Hill back as the deep man on the kick-return team. Hill was a twelfth-round draft pick from Georgia Tech in 1979 and had been used as a kick returner, averaging 20.1 yards a return in his rookie season.

Eddie Murray of Detroit sent a high, booming kick toward the Rams' goal line. Hill took the ball at his two-yard line and started upfield. He dodged tacklers at the 20 and found himself in the clear as he neared midfield. No one came close to Hill during the last 30 yards as he sped across the goal line for a touchdown.

On the very first play of the season the Rams had a 6–0 lead. It was the first time in four years that a Ram player had run a kick back for a score.

Unfortunately for the Rams, that was the high point of the day. The Lions, behind rookie Billy Sims, rolled to a 41–20 win. Still, Drew Hill had given the Rams and their fans a breathtaking start.

DALLAS' M&M BOYS

One was a home-grown Texas star, playing college ball at Southern Methodist University; the other was from the University of California. One was flashy and colorful, the other low-key and publicity-shy. Together they gave the Dallas Cowboys some of the best quarterbacking in the NFL in the 1960s and early 1970s. Their names were Don Meredith and Craig Morton.

Meredith was with the Cowboys when the team first started, sharing quarterbacking duties with Eddie LeBaron. The tiny LeBaron, only 5-foot-7, led the team in passing during its first three years before Meredith took over in 1963. Before he retired, LeBaron set the Dallas record of five TD passes in a game on October 21, 1962, in a 42–27 win over Pittsburgh.

The showy Meredith led the team in passing the next six years and three times tied LeBaron's record—against the New York Giants on September 18, 1966, and against the Philadelphia Eagles

Dallas' Dandy Don Meredith in one of his five-TD-pass games, against the New York Giants.

twice, on October 9, 1966, and on September 29, 1968. Sitting on the bench while Meredith was performing his feats was a young quarterback named Craig Morton.

Morton set passing records at California before Dallas drafted him as their number 1 pick in 1965. Craig took over the signal-calling job after Meredith retired, and the Cowboys continued their winning ways. On October 19, 1969, Morton passed his way into the Cowboy record book when he fired five TD passes against the Eagles. A year later Morton did it again, throwing for five TD's against Houston on December 20, 1970.

Meredith, known as Dandy Don, became a leading football commentator as well as a star in television commercials. Morton moved on to the Giants and the Denver Broncos.

But the M&M boys, and little Eddie, would share forever—or at least until somebody breaks it—the Dallas record for most touchdown passes in a game.

THE WALLOP OF A PACKER

"Jim Taylor has a great appetite for carrying the football. It's sort of a craving, a hunger—the most unusual thing I've ever seen in football."

So said Bart Starr in the days when he was quarterback of the Green Bay Packers and his fullback was a 5-foot-11, 212-pound running machine named Jim Taylor.

Before he carried a football, Jim had carried newspapers as a youngster in Baton Rouge, Louisiana. He went on to summer jobs, swinging a sledgehammer for offshore oil rigs in the Gulf of Mexico, all the while building himself up for football challenges at Louisiana State University and then at Green Bay, Wisconsin.

As a Packer, beginning in 1959, he was a bruising runner, the best fullback in the NFL for nearly a decade. Along the way he was voted the Most Valuable Player, when he led the Packers to the 1965 NFL championship over the Cleveland Browns. He scored the touchdown that gave Green Bay the lead

Green Bay's Jim Taylor, carrying against San Francisco in 1962, posted 19 touchdowns that year.

in the first Super Bowl, against Kansas City, in 1967.

It was in 1962, though, that Taylor put his name in the record book. On December 16 he scored a touchdown against Los Angeles that gave him a record total of 19 rushing touchdowns for the season. Since then only Earl Campbell of Houston, in 1979, and Chuck Muncie of San Diego, in 1981, have been able to match that total.

RAIDER SHARP-SHOOTER

As the 1969 season neared its climax, Daryle Lamonica was riding high. The quarterback from Notre Dame had led the Oakland Raiders to their third straight AFL Western Division title with 12 wins, one loss, and one tie. He had set a pro record by throwing six touchdown passes in the first half of a 50–21 victory over Buffalo.

The Raiders had stopped their archrivals, the Kansas City Chiefs, twice during the regular season, and would have to beat them again to win a trip to the Super Bowl. The AFL had a new playoff format in which the champion of the Eastern Division met the runner-up of the Western Division and the champion of the Western Division played the runner-up of the Eastern Division. The Chiefs qualified for the AFL title game by upsetting the Jets at New York on December 20, and the next day it was the Raiders' turn, against the Houston Oilers, who had qualified with an unimpressive 6-6-2 record. They met at Oakland-Alameda County Stadium.

Lamonica and company wasted no time, roaring off to a 28–0 lead in the first 10 minutes of the game. The field was muddy and the ball slippery, so Lamonica threw only 17 passes all day, completing 13. But six of those 13 completions went for touchdowns—two each to Fred Biletnikoff and Rod Sherman, and one apiece to Charlie Smith and Billy Cannon.

When the Raiders had completed their 56–7 rout, Lamonica praised his pass protection, calling it the best he ever had. And he welcomed facing Kansas City again. "Don't worry about us not being up for them," he said. "Everything rides on this game."

But the Raiders had ridden out their luck against Kansas City, and the Chiefs made off with a 17–7 victory, continuing on to beat Minnesota in Super Bowl IV.

So the season ended in disappointment for Daryle Lamonica. But on December 21 he had done something no other quarterback has ever accomplished—a six-touchdown game in post-season play.

THE TURKEY TROT

The Detroit Lions and the Chicago Bears were playing on Thanksgiving Day, 1980, and the game went into overtime tied at 17–17. The Bears won the all-important coin toss and elected to receive. Chicago's Dave Williams went back to receive Ed Murray's kick at the Pontiac, Michigan, Silverdome.

Williams had played quarterback in college at Colorado and had also been a member of the track team, running the 100-yard dash in 9.7 seconds. But when he was drafted, pro scouts saw him not as a quarterback but as a running back and kick-return specialist. And Williams was good at both jobs, scoring seven touchdowns in limited action in three pro seasons, beginning in 1977.

As Williams waited for the sudden-death overtime kickoff, one of the officials came over and said, "Sure hope this is over soon." He was looking forward to his Thanksgiving turkey.

Williams' answer came when he took Murray's

kick at the five-yard line and was going full speed by the time he reached the 20. It was no contest. The Bears' sprinter broke through a crowd of tacklers at the 25 and was untouched for the last 50 yards of a 95–yard touchdown run.

Williams' startling effort ended the NFL's shortest overtime game ever (21 seconds) and knocked the Lions out of the playoff race by a 23–17 score. It was Dave's third career kick-return TD, and it got the hungry official and everybody else home in time for turkey.

CRAZYLEGS

He was known as Crazylegs and it was the perfect description—his legs seemed to spin in six directions at once.

But Elroy (Crazylegs) Hirsch had the speed of a sprinter and a flair for spectacular over-the-head catches, and it was this combination that got him into the record book.

His home town was Wausau, Wisconsin. He began his football career at the University of Wisconsin in 1942, was shifted to Michigan in 1943, and became a star halfback at both schools. He was outstanding as well in baseball, basketball, and track and field.

After the war he played professionally with the Chicago Rockets in the All-American Football Conference, but injuries, including a fractured skull, seemed to end his career in the late 1940s.

But he came back in 1950 with the Los Angeles Rams and began a new life as an offensive end. It took him a season to learn his new position—to fake

Los Angeles' Elroy Hirsch, readying for a fingertip catch against Cleveland in the 1951 championship game, had 17 touchdowns on passes that season.

out the defenders, to change speeds, and to master all the complex pass patterns.

In 1951 it all paid off as the Rams won the NFL title. Crazylegs, with his fingertip catches, scored 17 touchdowns on passes to tie the NFL one-season record set by Don Hutson of Green Bay in 1942. Since then only one other receiver, Houston's Bill Groman in 1961, has caught that many TD passes in a season.

Hirsch finished his distinguished career in 1957, was elected to the College Football Hall of Fame, and eventually wound up at his old school, Wisconsin, where he is the athletic director.

TOSSING A SEVEN

Joe Kapp didn't go the normal route into the National Football League after playing college football at the University of California. As a quarterback, he'd led the Golden Bears to the Pacific Coast Conference title in 1958 and a berth in the Rose Bowl. But after graduation he chose to play football professionally in the Canadian Football League.

After several seasons north of the border, he and coach Bud Grant wound up with the Minnesota Vikings. In their second season there, 1968, they helped change the Vikings from a last-place team to one that won the NFL's Central Division title. Kapp's passes, though often wobbly, were usually on target. And he was a fiery leader whose drive and spirit had a winning effect on the Vikings.

Early in the 1969 season—on September 28—the Vikings were at home against the defending champion Baltimore Colts. Kapp proceeded to find holes in the Baltimore secondary, throwing passes that simply destroyed the Colts. By the time the game was over, Kapp had connected seven times on touchdown passes—twice to Gene Washington and once each to Dave Osborn, Bob Grim, Kent Kramer, John Beasley, and Jim Lindsey. The final score of 52–14 was not nearly as important as Kapp's performance.

By heaving seven TD passes, Kapp had tied the NFL one-game record shared by Sid Luckman of the Chicago Bears, Y.A. Tittle of the New York Giants, George Blanda of the Houston Oilers, and Adrian Burk of the Philadelphia Eagles.

Strangely enough, Burk was on the field as an official when Kapp tied Burk's record.

AN UNLIKELY HERO

It was only the opening game of the 1980 season, but excitement ran high. When the Green Bay Packers and the Chicago Bears tangle, the contest has special meaning. They have been rivals since 1923.

And this game at Green Bay on September 7 was the usual hard-hitting affair, with the defenses dominating. The teams moved into overtime tied at 6–6, but now it looked as if the Packers were about to break through. Quarterback Lynn Dickey started a drive toward the goal early in overtime. Mixing passes to James Lofton with runs by Eddie Lee Ivery, the Packers moved to the Bears' 18-yard line. This was within field-goal range for Chester Marcol, the team's bespectacled kicker.

When the drive stalled, Bart Starr sent Marcol into the game for a 35-yard attempt. The ball was snapped. Marcol kicked it—right into the middle of the Bears' line! Chicago's Alan Page slapped the ball back, and, in a million-to-one shot, it bounced directly back into Marcol's hands. The kicker reacted instinctively—he ran. And, since most of the Bears had fallen after trying to block the kick, Marcol realized that he might be able to run for a first down and keep the Packers' drive alive.

He did even better. Taking off to his left, Marcol outran a few linemen and was suddenly in the clear. With a pack of frustrated Bears behind him, Marcol sped down the sideline and raced into the end zone. Touchdown! Green Bay's Lambeau Field exploded. The Packers had won, 12–6, and had an unlikely hero: a kicker who ran 25 yards for the winning score in overtime.

HEROES OF THE HEISMAN

Marcus Allen, the first in college football history to gain more than 2,000 yards in a season, flew in a 747 jumbo jet to New York City in December 1981 to accept an award at the Downtown Athletic Club. It was a secret until it was announced on a nationally televised program that the University of Southern California tailback had won the prized Heisman Trophy.

Forty-six years earlier Jay Berwanger, a running back from the University of Chicago, flew in an airplane for the first time, a propeller-driven craft that took longer to get from Chicago to New York than it did Marcus Allen from California.

But both made their flights for the same reason. Each had been voted college football's outstanding player of the year.

Berwanger, in 1935, was the first winner of the award that was named in honor of a star college player at Brown and Penn who coached football for nearly 40 years, including 16 at Georgia Tech, where his teams were undefeated in 1915, 1916, and 1917.

Most of the winners of the 25-pound trophy have been quarterbacks and running backs. Only two linemen have ever been chosen, and both were pass-catching ends—Larry Kelley of Yale and Leon Hart of Notre Dame.

All knew their way to the end zone. Some went on to careers in the professional game, some to other jobs. Winning the Heisman is no guarantee of success in the world from then on.

But one thing they all have in common, said Brigadier General Pete Dawkins, the 1958 winner from Army, is that deep down they're not sure they deserve it. But nobody has yet given the trophy back.

Southern California's Marcus Allen won the Heisman Trophy in 1981.

HEISMAN TROPHY WINNERS

1935 Jay Berwanger, Chicago, halfback (HB)
1936 Larry Kelley, Yale, end (E)
1937 Clint Frank, Yale, quarterback (QB)
1938 Davey O'Brien, Texas Christian, QB
1939 Nile Kinnick, Iowa, QB
1940 Tom Harmon, Michigan, HB
1941 Bruce Smith, Minnesota, HB
1942 Frank Sinkwich, Georgia, HB
1943 Angelo Bertelli, Notre Dame, QB
1944 Les Horvath, Ohio State, QB
1945 Doc Blanchard, Army, fullback (FB)
1946 Glenn Davis, Army, HB
1947 John Lujack, Notre Dame, QB
1948 Doak Walker, Southern Methodist, HB
1949 Leon Hart, Notre Dame, E
1950 Vic Janowicz, Ohio State, HB
1951 Dick Kazmaier, Princeton, HB
1952 Billy Vessels, Oklahoma, HB
1953 John Lattner, Notre Dame, HB
1954 Alan Ameche, Wisconsin, FB
1955 Howard Cassady, Ohio State, HB
1956 Paul Hornung, Notre Dame, QB
1957 John David Crow, Texas A&M, HB
1958 Pete Dawkins, Army, HB
1959 Billy Cannon, Louisiana State, HB
1960 Joe Bellino, Navy, HB
1961 Ernie Davis, Syracuse, HB
1962 Terry Baker, Oregon State, QB
1963 Roger Staubach, Navy, QB
1964 John Huarte, Notre Dame, QB
1965 Mike Garrett, Southern California, HB
1966 Steve Spurrier, Florida, QB
1967 Gary Beban, UCLA, QB
1968 O.J. Simpson, Southern California, running back (RB)

1969 Steve Owens, Oklahoma, RB
1970 Jim Plunkett, Stanford, QB
1971 Pat Sullivan, Auburn, QB
1972 Johnny Rodgers, Nebraska, RB
1973 John Cappelletti, Penn State, RB
1974 Archie Griffin, Ohio State, RB
1975 Archie Griffin, Ohio State, RB
1976 Tony Dorsett, Pittsburgh, RB
1977 Earl Campbell, Texas, RB
1978 Billy Sims, Oklahoma, RB
1979 Charles White, Southern California, RB
1980 George Rogers, South Carolina, RB
1981 Marcus Allen, Southern California, RB

THE PRICE OF FAME

As police officer Joe Coffey on television's *Hill Street Blues,* Ed Marinaro is an actor who has had the benefit of a strong supporting cast. But as an All-American running back at Cornell, Ed Marinaro was the whole show.

A native of New Milford, New Jersey, Marinaro was such an outstanding all-around athlete in high school that he was recruited to play basketball, not football, at Cornell.

During his three varsity football seasons with the Big Red (1969, 1970, and 1971), Marinaro was a workhorse who scored 52 touchdowns in 27 games, a National Collegiate Athletic Association (NCAA) record average of 1.93 touchdowns per game. Along the way Marinaro set records for average yards per game over a single season with 209 and over a career with 174.6. And he was named the Ivy League's Player of the Era.

Perhaps his most memorable effort came in the fourth game of his college career. Marinaro scored five touchdowns against Harvard and gained 281 yards on a whopping 40 carries for a 41–24 Cornell victory on October 18, 1969.

"I enjoy carrying the ball a lot," said Marinaro, who went on to play in the pros with the Minnesota Vikings, New York Jets, and Seattle Seahawks. "When the game is over I hurt all over. But after a victory, it's worth it—sort of the price you have to pay."

This was the day in 1969 when Cornell's Ed Marinaro scored five touchdowns against Harvard.

A RARE FRESHMAN

Herschel Walker began his college career in 1980 standing on the sidelines, holding his helmet and watching a couple of ordinary University of Georgia tailbacks carry the ball against the Tennessee Volunteers. Georgia Bulldog coach Vince Dooley, realizing that the eyes of all the fans would be focused on his prize freshman running back, had decided to protect Walker from the glare of the opening-day spotlight on September 16 at Tennessee's Neyland Stadium.

By the time halftime rolled around, Walker still hadn't gotten his uniform dirty, and Georgia was on the wrong end of a 15–0 score. Dooley couldn't keep his biggest weapon under wraps any longer. After Georgia scored a safety, Walker got his chance. He took a handoff at the Vols' 16, ran over a defensive lineman at the 10, and then blasted his way through two more defenders who tried to sandwich him at the five. Touchdown!

Later that afternoon Walker added another score

Georgia's Herschel Walker, scoring here against Vanderbilt, ended up with 15 touchdowns as a freshman in 1980.

from eight yards out to give Georgia a 16–15 victory. Georgia, led by Walker, was on its way to a perfect 12-0 record and the national championship.

Walker shattered the freshman rushing record set by Pitt's Tony Dorsett, accumulating 1,616 yards with his combination of speed, strength, and finesse. And when it came to getting six points, no freshman rusher ever did it more often. Walker's three-touchdown performance against Georgia Tech gave him 15 for the season—the most rushing touchdowns scored by a freshman in NCAA history.

A HISTORY LESSON

Lydell Mitchell was a history major at Penn State, and when he wasn't studying, he was making history on the football field.

Mitchell grew up in Salem, New Jersey, where he was his high-school class president. He began his college playing career as a halfback in 1969. He showed great promise, scoring six touchdowns for the Nittany Lions in each of his first two seasons, but it was in his senior year that he burst out like a comet.

One of his teammates was Franco Harris, who would go on to greater fame as a star of the Pittsburgh Steelers. Mitchell and Harris led Penn State on a winning streak that reached 15 games before it was snapped by Tennessee on December 4, 1971.

By then Mitchell, who had twice scored four touchdowns in a game, owned all sorts of NCAA major-college one-season records, including most touchdowns scored (29), most touchdowns scored rushing (26), and most points scored (174).

The 6-foot, 200-pounder always insisted that "records are nice, but winning is nicer." But he added that "if there are no records to be broken, there is not much sense in competing."

MR. INSIDE AND MR. OUTSIDE

They were an unbeatable combination. They were known in college football as Mr. Inside and Mr. Outside, and they were running backs at the United States Military Academy, commonly called Army and located at West Point in New York State.

Mr. Inside was Felix (Doc) Blanchard, who was born in Bishopville, South Carolina. His father was a doctor, hence his nickname. Mr. Outside was Glenn Davis, who came to West Point from Claremont, California.

Davis, whose specialty was to run to the outside of his offensive line, began his Army career in 1943, scoring eight touchdowns for the Cadets. When Blanchard came along in 1944, West Point took off on a three-year unbeaten streak that few schools have matched. The Cadets were 27-0-1 in those years, with only a scoreless tie against Notre Dame in 1946 to spoil the record.

During that time Davis was virtually unstoppable. The slippery Mr. Outside recorded 59

Glenn Davis (left) and Doc Blanchard powered Army with military precision.

touchdowns, 43 on runs, 14 on pass receptions, and two on punt returns. Davis' record for TD's in a four-year, major-college career stood by itself until Pitt's Tony Dorsett tied it in 1976.

At the same time Blanchard, who was best at running on the inside of his offensive line, was pounding away for 38 touchdowns, and between them Blanchard and Davis made 10 of Army's touchdowns in three winning games against their archenemy, Navy.

Blanchard later became an air force flier and was decorated when he piloted his burning plane to a safe landing, refusing to bail out lest the plane crash in a populated area.

Davis served three years as an infantry officer, resigning in 1950 to join the Los Angeles Rams. An injury kept him from hitting his true stride as a pro and he quit the sport for a promotion job with the Los Angeles *Times*.

But for those years during World War II, Mr. Inside and Mr. Outside were an attack force at West Point that brought excitement to all who followed them.

THE GALLOPING GHOST

They nicknamed him the Iceman because he delivered ice in the summer; they called him Red because of his hair; but he was best known as the Galloping Ghost because of the way he eluded tacklers while carrying a football.

Harold Grange, whose father was the burly boss of a lumber camp, enrolled at the University of Illinois in 1922 after a spectacular high-school career in Wheaton, Illinois. He weighed only 166 pounds and no doubt wondered about his chances against all the big guys.

He didn't have to wonder long. As a sophomore in 1923, wearing the number 77 that he would make famous, Red was a starter in the opening game against Nebraska. He scored all of his team's touchdowns in a 24–7 victory.

In 1923 and 1924, Illinois won every game but two (one loss and one tie). Grange's greatest day came on a hot Saturday in October 1924 against Michigan. On the opening kickoff Grange bolted 92 yards for a touchdown. A few minutes later he broke loose for another, a twisting, dodging 70-yard run. Soon after, Red added a third TD on a 57-yard sprint, and then a fourth of 43 yards. All this happened in the first 12 minutes of the game.

Nobody kept track of such things, but this may have been a record for most touchdowns by a player in the shortest amount of time. He ran for one more touchdown later in the game. And he threw for another. Illinois won, 39–14, and Grange had either run or passed for all six Illinois touchdowns.

Grange joined the Chicago Bears of the National Football League after graduation and became the first superstar of professional football.

But he will be remembered most for that glorious afternoon when he was, indeed, the Galloping Ghost against Michigan.

So far, no one has topped Red Grange's four touchdowns in one quarter for Illinois in 1924.

SHOWBOAT

When Arnold Boykin showed up on the campus of the University of Mississippi, he already had a nickname, Showboat.

How did he get it? "By showing off," he wrote on the questionnaire given him by the school's sports public relations office.

At Greenville High School in Mississippi, Boykin had starred in football, basketball, and track, and he was looked on as a prime prospect at Ole Miss. Ice cream was his favorite food and math his favorite subject. Football was his favorite sport.

He had played quarterback, guard, and fullback at Greenville and would end up as a fullback in the Rebels' offense. But he suffered injuries—knee and ankle—during his sophomore and junior years and had trouble living up to his potential.

Going into the final game of 1951, his senior year, Boykin had scored only three touchdowns for the season. Mississippi's opponent was its archrival, Mississippi State, playing at home in Starkville.

That day, December 1, Showboat lived up to his nickname. When quarterback Jim Lear wasn't calling pass plays, Boykin was running the ball. He ran it for touchdowns seven times—on runs of 14, 12, 17, 13, 85, 1, and 5 yards. Ole Miss routed Mississippi State, 49–7, to win the "Golden Egg," a mounted gold football that went back and forth between these traditional rivals.

The seven touchdowns put Showboat in the record book. They represented the most touchdowns ever scored by one man in an NCAA major-college game.

THE CARLISLE INDIAN

The legend of Jim Thorpe has all the ingredients of a fairy tale. It begins with the most unusual of all football teams, the Carlisle Indians. Their coach, Glenn (Pop) Warner, once said of Carlisle: "As a school, it had no traditions, but what the Indians did have was a very real race pride and a fierce determination to show the palefaces what they could do when the odds were even."

Starting in 1900, for 15 years, this tiny Pennsylvania college played, and usually defeated, all the major universities—Yale, Harvard, Penn, and any others who dared compete against them. And the greatest Carlisle Indian of them all was the one named Jim Thorpe.

An all-around athlete, Thorpe was so outstanding in track and field, he swept the pentathlon and decathlon competition at the 1912 Olympic Games in Stockholm, Sweden. That was when King Gustav V of Sweden said to him: "Sir, you are the greatest athlete in the world."

Carlisle's Jim Thorpe was the greatest athlete of his time.

It was in the fall of 1912 that Thorpe was at his peak as a Carlisle football player, scoring 25 touchdowns that season. One of his best performances came against an Army team that included a young cadet named Dwight D. Eisenhower. Forty years later Eisenhower would be President of the United States. On that day in 1912 he and his fellow cadets couldn't contain Thorpe, who ran for two touchdowns as Carlisle whipped Army, 27–6.

Thorpe later played pro football and even had a big-league baseball career. But it was on the gridiron that he had no equal. In 1951 this Sac and Fox Indian was named "the greatest football player of the half-century" by an Associated Press poll.

SOONER IN A RUSH

In Miami, Oklahoma, where Steve Owens grew up one of nine children, he was already a hero to the many Oklahoma football fans.

Entering his senior year at the University of Oklahoma in 1969, this 6-foot-3, 215-pound halfback had scored 33 touchdowns and was a preseason All-America choice.

He'd been relatively free of injuries, and there were those who wondered whether he'd remain unhurt in his final season. He seemed quietly confident. "I believe in physical conditioning," he said. "And I believe in going full speed every time, hitting them harder than they hit you."

Owens was certainly in good shape and he hit hardest in 1969. He pounded out 23 touchdowns in that year alone. When they added it all up, he had scored 56 touchdowns on rushing attempts for an NCAA major-college record.

It was not unexpected when, shortly after the season ended, he was voted winner of the Heisman Trophy as college football's Player of the Year.

T.D. SAYS IT ALL

A weary, grimy-looking man approached Tony Dorsett's car. It was Tony's junior year in high school and the first time he had picked up his father at the steel mill in Aliquippa, Pennsylvania, where the elder Dorsett worked.

"My dad had always told me not to get stuck in a steel mill and that day convinced me," said Dorsett. "I made up my mind right there that I would rather be a football player."

Dorsett left the steel mills far behind when he became the greatest running back in University of Pittsburgh history. Dorsett matched Army's Glenn Davis for the most career touchdowns scored by a college player with 59, including 55 rushing. He set an NCAA scoring record by adding a two-point conversion for a career total of 356 points. In a four-year, 44-game Pitt career, he gained an NCAA-record 6,082 yards rushing and had 33 games of at least 100 yards each. Dorsett, a compact 5-foot-11, began his Pitt career as a 155-pound freshman who gained 101 yards in the opening game of the 1973 season. He finished it as a 195-pound Heisman Trophy winner who gained 224 yards and scored two touchdowns against Penn State in 1976.

Dorsett, nicknamed the Hawk by his father because of his wide-set eyes, came to be known by his initials during his outstanding years at Pitt and later with the NFL Dallas Cowboys. And they couldn't have been more fitting for a football player—T.D.

Pitt's Tony Dorsett racked up 59 touchdowns from 1973 through 1976.

KID FLIPPERS IN COLLEGE

The University of Florida Gators had a veteran team in the 1969 season—except at quarterback. They were trusting their signal-calling duties to an untested sophomore named John Reaves. The Gators were uncertain how he'd respond as they took the field on September 20 for their opener against the University of Houston at Gators Stadium.

Three hours later their doubts had been erased. The Gators had destroyed Houston, 59–34, and Reaves had had the greatest game ever played by a first-time college quarterback. He threw five touchdown passes, an NCAA record for a quarterback in his first game.

Purdue's Mark Herrmann also broke in with a bang, but over the course of a season rather than in his opening game. As a freshman in 1977, Herrmann set a major-college record when he passed for 18 touchdowns. Herrmann and Reaves have something else in common: the major-college record for passes attempted in a career. Herrmann holds the four-year record with 1,218 and Reaves the three-year mark with 1,128.

LIGHTNING STRIKES TWICE

Anthony Davis moved back toward his goal line and waited for the kick. It was December 2, 1972, and his University of Southern California (USC) team was battling Notre Dame at the Los Angeles Coliseum. It was a game USC had to win if it was to keep its ranking as the nation's number 1 team.

Davis made sure USC would get off to a good start: he took the opening kickoff at his own three-yard line and raced up the left sideline. He broke into the clear, faked the last man off his feet, and sped into the end zone for a 97-yard touchdown run.

USC had the early lead, but Notre Dame kept coming back. With the score USC 25, Notre Dame 23, the Irish kicked off in the third quarter. Davis fielded the kickoff at his three and headed downfield. Suddenly he was in the open. He broke two tackles around midfield and then it was clear sailing to his second kick-return TD of the day.

Southern California's Anthony Davis returned six kicks for touchdowns from 1972 through 1974.

Davis, then only a sophomore, returned four more kicks for touchdowns over the course of his career. His total of six kick-return TD's is an NCAA record.

A PASSING SEASON

As far as Brigham Young's Jim McMahon and Portland State's Neil Lomax were concerned, 1980 was the year of the passer in college football.

McMahon, a quarterback like Lomax, threw 47 touchdown passes (an NCAA record) in 12 games, almost four a game.

At Portland State, Lomax ended a brilliant three-year career by passing for 37 touchdowns as a senior, running his college total up to 106, another NCAA record.

Lomax had perhaps the greatest day of any college quarterback on November 8, 1980, in Portland. Playing against Delaware State, he threw seven TD passes in the first quarter. He scored once himself and passed for another score in the third quarter before taking a seat on the bench. His eight TD passes set a record as Portland State crushed Delaware State, 105–0.

Lomax became a second-round draft choice of

the NFL's St. Louis Cardinals in 1980. As a rookie he saw little action, but in 1981 he shared the quarterbacking assignment with veteran Jim Hart and seemed on the way to full-time duty in the signal-caller's spot.

McMahon as a senior in 1981 continued to set school, Western Athletic Conference, and NCAA records. And he finished third behind USC's Marcus Allen and South Carolina's Herschel Walker in the balloting for the Heisman Trophy.

Brigham Young's Jim McMahon passed for 47 TD's in 1980.

THE CUMBERLAND MASSACRE

It all started with an innocent little offer of a $500 guarantee to tiny Cumberland College if it would play powerful Georgia Tech in Atlanta.

Since there was no football manager at the Lebanon, Tennessee, school when the invitation arrived in spring 1915, it wound up in the hands of a senior football player named M.S. McGregor. He promptly accepted the invitation for Cumberland, but since he was graduated in June he wasn't around to see the results.

By the fall George Allen had become Cumberland's football manager. His chief responsibilities were to make sure the school fielded a team in Atlanta on October 7 and to collect its $500 after the game. Allen had to suit up several non-students, some of whom had never played football before. Even so, the Cumberland team that showed up to play Tech that day had only 16 players, including a few injured regulars.

Cumberland realized it was in trouble early. For

Georgia Tech's Yellow Jackets, touchdowns flowed freely. Georgia Tech halfback Everett Strupper scored seven times and was headed for an eighth late in the game when he good-naturedly downed the ball on the Cumberland one-yard line.

Even Georgia Tech's lumbering right guard, Canty Alexander, got in on the fun. Alexander, who had never scored a TD in his college career, was promised by his teammates that they'd get him one. He set up in the backfield and the ball was snapped, but it bounced off his chest. He was still able to pick it up and bring it over for his touchdown.

It was that kind of day for Cumberland. Although the second half was shortened from 30 to 17½ minutes by mutual agreement, the game seemed endless for Cumberland. By the time it was over, Georgia Tech had set records for the most points, most yards gained (978), most players scoring touchdowns (13), most points after touchdowns by one player (18), and most points in a quarter (63, twice). The final score? Georgia Tech 222, Cumberland 0.

THE OLDEST BOWL OF ALL

It is the granddaddy of the Bowl games. It dates back to the end of the 1901 season, when students at Stanford University in Palo Alto, California, issued a challenge to the team from the University of Michigan, considered the best in the country that year. It was called the East–West Game then. That first one was played on January 1, 1902, at Tournament Park in Pasadena, California.

It turned out to be a slaughter. Even though touchdowns were worth only five points in those days, the Wolverines wound up winning, 49–0.

There wasn't another East–West Game until 1916, and it wasn't until 1923 that it officially became the Rose Bowl Game, when a specially built stadium, called the Rose Bowl, seating more than 100,000, was built in Pasadena.

This New Year's Day annual has had many memorable touchdowns. For sheer distance, none rivals a kickoff return by UCLA's Al Hoisch in the 1947 game against Illinois.

Hoisch, a substitute halfback, took a kickoff three yards deep into his own end zone, started out for the right sideline, faked his way past several defenders, and followed his blockers until he had only three men to beat at midfield. Cutting sharply, Hoisch left the Illinois players trailing him and raced into the end zone. Though Illinois won the game, 45–14, Hoisch's 103-yard kickoff return stands as the longest scoring run in a Rose Bowl.

The 1963 contest between Wisconsin and USC is considered one of the most exciting in Rose Bowl history. It featured a pair of strong-armed quarterbacks at the peak of their explosiveness. USC's Pete Beathard completed a 57-yard touchdown pass to Hal Bedsole on his team's first play from scrimmage. Beathard added three more scoring passes to set a Rose Bowl record of four. Bedsole caught a second TD pass to make him one of seven receivers to share the record for most TD receptions in a Rose Bowl game.

Wisconsin quarterback Ron VanderKelen was almost as hard to beat as Beathard, throwing 48 times, including two TD passes, to lead his team back from a 42–17 deficit. The Wisconsin comeback fell short, 42–37, but no Rose Bowl game has featured as many touchdown passes—six.

USC's Sam Cunningham holds the post–World War II record for rushing touchdowns with four—none from more than five yards out—against Ohio State in 1973. Michigan's Neil Snow barreled over for five in the 1902 game against Stanford.

USC's Jim Hardy accounted for the most career Rose Bowl TD's, throwing for five and running for one as the Trojans beat Washington in 1944 and Tennessee in 1945.

In 1925, Notre Dame's Elmer Layden intercepted a Stanford pass and returned it 78 yards for the longest Rose Bowl touchdown by interception.

ROSE BOWL RESULTS

1902	Michigan 49, Stanford 0
1916	Washington State 14, Brown 0
1917	Oregon 14, Pennsylvania 0
1920	Harvard 7, Oregon 6
1921	California 28, Ohio State 0
1922	California 0, Washington & Jefferson 0
1923	Southern California 14, Penn State 3
1924	Navy 14, Washington 14
1925	Notre Dame 27, Stanford 10
1926	Alabama 20, Washington 19
1927	Alabama 7, Stanford 7
1928	Stanford 7, Pittsburgh 6
1929	Georgia Tech 8, California 7
1930	Southern California 47, Pittsburgh 14
1931	Alabama 24, Washington State 0
1932	Southern California 21, Tulane 12
1933	Southern California 35, Pittsburgh 0
1934	Columbia 7, Stanford 0
1935	Alabama 29, Stanford 13
1936	Stanford 7, Southern Methodist 0
1937	Pittsburgh 21, Washington 0
1938	California 13, Alabama 0
1939	Southern California 7, Duke 3
1940	Southern California 14, Tennessee 0

1941	Stanford 21, Nebraska 13
1942	Oregon State 20, Duke 16
1943	Georgia 9, UCLA 0
1944	Southern California 29, Washington 0
1945	Southern California 25, Tennessee 0
1946	Alabama 34, Southern California 14
1947	Illinois 45, UCLA 14
1948	Michigan 49, Southern California 0
1949	Northwestern 20, California 14
1950	Ohio State 17, California 14
1951	Michigan 14, California 6
1952	Illinois 40, Stanford 7
1953	Southern California 7, Wisconsin 0
1954	Michigan State 28, UCLA 20
1955	Ohio State 20, Southern California 7
1956	Michigan State 17, UCLA 14
1957	Iowa 35, Oregon State 19
1958	Ohio State 10, Oregon 7
1959	Iowa 38, California 12
1960	Washington 44, Wisconsin 8
1961	Washington 17, Minnesota 7
1962	Minnesota 21, UCLA 3
1963	Southern California 42, Wisconsin 37
1964	Illinois 17, Washington 7
1965	Michigan 34, Oregon State 7
1966	UCLA 14, Michigan State 12
1967	Purdue 14, Southern California 13
1968	Southern California 14, Indiana 3
1969	Ohio State 27, Southern California 16
1970	Southern California 10, Michigan 3
1971	Stanford 27, Ohio State 17
1972	Stanford 13, Michigan 12
1973	Southern California 42, Ohio State 17
1974	Ohio State 42, Southern California 21
1975	Southern California 18, Ohio State 17
1976	UCLA 23, Ohio State 10

1977	Southern California 14, Michigan 6
1978	Washington 27, Michigan 20
1979	Southern California 17, Michigan 10
1980	Southern California 17, Ohio State 16
1981	Michigan 23, Washington 6
1982	Washington 28, Iowa 0

OFF-THE-BENCH BOWL

To the football world Dallas means the NFL Cowboys, but Dallas is also home of the Cotton Bowl, where since 1937 the great stars and teams of college football have played on New Year's Day. And where in 1954 a very odd thing occurred.

It was late in the first half and Rice led Alabama, 7–6. Bart Starr, the Alabama quarterback, had fumbled and now Rice had the ball on its own five-yard line. The quarterback barked the signals for play "47F." The F meant that the fullback was to fake a carry into the middle of the line. The 47 meant that Dicky Moegle, Rice's star halfback, was to get the ball and try to sweep around right end.

This was a dangerous tactic for a team trapped in its own territory. If Alabama figured out the play correctly, Moegle might be driven into his own end zone. That would give Alabama a safety, adding two points and giving the Crimson Tide an 8–7 lead.

But the Rice quarterback was guessing right that

40

day. The fullback's fake deceived Alabama. Moegle then swept around his right end and headed down the sideline. He seemed to be flying as he shot past the chalk lines that marked the five-yard intervals.

The crowd of 75,000 suddenly came alive to the possibility of a 95-yard touchdown run. Moegle was outdistancing his blockers as well as opposition tacklers as he approached midfield. Only one defensive back stood any chance of catching the Rice speedster. And that back would have to come from the middle of the field as Moegle sped near the Alabama bench along the sideline.

The players on the bench, among them fullback Tommy Lewis, who had scored the Alabama touchdown, were helpless as Moegle raced by.

Then it happened. Suddenly Lewis leaped off the bench and cut Moegle down with a perfect tackle. Moegle tumbled to earth on the 38-yard line and looked at Lewis in amazement. Alabama's twelfth man on the field retreated to the bench almost as quickly as he had come off it. The shocked spectators watched in disbelief.

Lewis sat down and buried his face in his hands. Referee Cliff Shaw, going by the rules, picked up the ball and carried it the rest of the way, giving Moegle credit for a 95-yard touchdown.

Lewis later explained: "I guess I'm too full of Alabama. He just ran too close. I didn't know what I was doing. After I pulled him down, I jumped up

Facing page, top: Watch 42, Alabama's Tommy Lewis, on the sidelines as Rice's Dicky Moegle runs past with the ball. Center: Lewis tackles Moegle. Bottom: Lewis, far right, prepares to head back to the bench.

and got back on the bench and kept telling myself: 'I didn't do it. I didn't do it.' But I knew I did."

Realizing that Lewis' tackle was simply a spontaneous expression of team pride, the officials allowed the fullback to remain in the game. Alabama needed every available player if it was to overtake Rice.

But Lewis' presence wasn't enough. Moegle, who had run 79 yards for Rice's first touchdown in the game, scored again on a 34-yard run in the third quarter. His teammate Buddy Grantham added another for a 28–6 victory. Moegle had gained 265 yards on 11 carries and scored three touchdowns. He was clearly the game's Most Valuable Player.

Tommy Lewis got no award, but because of one impulsive tackle, he and Dicky Moegle would be forever linked in football history.

COTTON BOWL RESULTS

1937	Texas Christian 16, Marquette 6
1938	Rice 28, Colorado 14
1939	St. Mary's 20, Texas Tech 13
1940	Clemson 6, Boston College 3
1941	Texas A&M 13, Fordham 12
1942	Alabama 29, Texas A&M 21
1943	Texas 14, Georgia Tech 7
1944	Randolph Field 7, Texas 7
1945	Oklahoma A&M 34, Texas Christian 0
1946	Texas 40, Missouri 27
1947	Arkansas 0, Louisiana State 0
1948	Southern Methodist 13, Penn State 13
1949	Southern Methodist 21, Oregon 13

1950	Rice 27, North Carolina 13
1951	Tennessee 20, Texas 14
1952	Kentucky 20, Texas Christian 7
1953	Texas 16, Tennessee 0
1954	Rice 28, Alabama 6
1955	Georgia Tech 14, Arkansas 6
1956	Mississippi 14, Texas Christian 13
1957	Texas Christian 28, Syracuse 27
1958	Navy 20, Rice 7
1959	Texas Christian 0, Air Force 0
1960	Syracuse 23, Texas 14
1961	Duke 7, Arkansas 6
1962	Texas 12, Mississippi 7
1963	Louisiana State 13, Texas 0
1964	Texas 28, Navy 6
1965	Arkansas 10, Nebraska 7
1966	Louisiana State 14, Arkansas 7
1967	Georgia 24, Southern Methodist 9
1968	Texas A&M 20, Alabama 16
1969	Texas 36, Tennessee 13
1970	Texas 21, Notre Dame 17
1971	Notre Dame 24, Texas 11
1972	Penn State 30, Texas 6
1973	Texas 17, Alabama 13
1974	Nebraska 19, Texas 3
1975	Penn State 41, Baylor 20
1976	Arkansas 31, Georgia 10
1977	Houston 30, Maryland 21
1978	Notre Dame 38, Texas 10
1979	Notre Dame 35, Houston 34
1980	Houston 17, Nebraska 14
1981	Alabama 30, Baylor 2
1982	Texas 14, Alabama 12

THE SWEETEST BOWL

Notre Dame desperately needed a lift. It was New Year's Eve, 1973, and the Fighting Irish were trailing Alabama, 7–6, in the Sugar Bowl in New Orleans. The winner would be declared national champion.

In the second quarter Notre Dame's Al Hunter went back to receive the Alabama kickoff. He knew the Irish needed a score before halftime because Alabama was usually very tough once it got the lead. Hunter took the high kick at his own seven-yard line and started upfield. He broke a tackle at the 20 and was suddenly in the clear. No one touched him the final 50 yards as Hunter completed a 93-yard touchdown run, the longest kick return in Sugar Bowl history. The score gave the Irish a 14–7 lead on the way to a hard-fought 24–23 triumph and the national title.

The Sugar Bowl, begun on New Year's Day, 1935, when Tulane met Temple, has had its share of dramatic touchdowns. Charley Trippi and Dan Edwards of Georgia teamed up on a 67-yard TD pass that sparked the Bulldogs' 20–10 win over North Carolina in 1947. That play, the longest TD reception in Sugar Bowl history, set the stage for Georgia to extend its winning streak to 16 games.

Bruce Bolton of Alabama made a diving circus catch of Jeff Rutledge's TD pass in 1979 to give the Crimson Tide a 14–7 win over Penn State and the national championship. In 1945, Hugh Morrow set a Sugar Bowl record with an interception return of 75 yards for a score, but Morrow's Alabama team lost to Duke, 29–26.

The longest TD run from scrimmage in the Sugar Bowl happened in 1958. Mississippi's Raymond Brown, standing in his end zone to punt, received a bad snap from center. But most of the Texas players had spun around and run downfield to block for the punt returner. Brown avoided tacklers near his five-yard line and took off. He never stopped until he crossed the Texas goal line, completing what went into the Sugar Bowl record book as a 92-yard touchdown. It was the last one in Ole Miss's 39–7 rout of the Longhorns.

SUGAR BOWL RESULTS

1935	Tulane 20, Temple 14
1936	Texas Christian 3, Louisiana State 2
1937	Santa Clara 21, Louisiana State 14

1938 Santa Clara 6, Louisiana State 0
1939 Texas Christian 15, Carnegie Tech 7
1940 Texas A&M 14, Tulane 13
1941 Boston College 19, Tennessee 13
1942 Fordham 2, Missouri 0
1943 Tennessee 14, Tulsa 7
1944 Georgia Tech 20, Tulsa 18
1945 Duke 29, Alabama 26
1946 Oklahoma A&M 33, St. Mary's 13
1947 Georgia 20, North Carolina 10
1948 Texas 27, Alabama 7
1949 Oklahoma 14, North Carolina 6
1950 Oklahoma 35, Louisiana State 0
1951 Kentucky 13, Oklahoma 7
1952 Maryland 28, Tennessee 13
1953 Georgia Tech 24, Mississippi 7
1954 Georgia Tech 42, West Virginia 19
1955 Navy 21, Mississippi 0
1956 Georgia Tech 7, Pittsburgh 0
1957 Baylor 13, Tennessee 7
1958 Mississippi 39, Texas 7
1959 Louisiana State 7, Clemson 0
1960 Mississippi 21, Louisiana State 0
1961 Mississippi 14, Rice 6
1962 Alabama 10, Arkansas 3
1963 Mississippi 17, Arkansas 13
1964 Alabama 12, Mississippi 7
1965 Louisiana State 13, Syracuse 10
1966 Missouri 20, Florida 18
1967 Alabama 34, Nebraska 7
1968 Louisiana State 20, Wyoming 13
1969 Arkansas 16, Georgia 2
1970 Mississippi 27, Arkansas 22
1971 Tennessee 34, Air Force 13
1972 Oklahoma 40, Auburn 22

1972*	Oklahoma 14, Penn State 0
1973	Notre Dame 24, Alabama 23
1974	Nebraska 13, Florida 10
1975	Alabama 13, Penn State 6
1977	Pittsburgh 27, Georgia 3
1978	Alabama 35, Ohio State 6
1979	Alabama 14, Penn State 7
1980	Alabama 24, Arkansas 9
1981	Georgia 17, Notre Dame 10
1982	Pittsburgh 24, Georgia 20

* The games from 1972 (Oklahoma–Penn State) through 1975 were played on December 31. All others were played on January 1. As a result there are two games listed for 1972 and none for 1976. Also, Oklahoma defeated Penn State, 14–0, in 1972 but Penn State was awarded the game by forfeit.

THE JUICIEST BOWL

The Orange Bowl in Miami, Florida, has been the site of many great individual performances since the first game in 1935, but none can top the one turned in by Nebraska's Johnny Rodgers in 1973.

Rodgers, who had returned a punt for 77 yards and a TD in Nebraska's 1972 Orange Bowl victory over Alabama, was a one-man wrecking crew against Notre Dame the following season. Rodgers scored on runs of eight, four, and five yards; caught a 50-yard TD pass from David Humm; and, for good measure, threw a 52-yard scoring strike to Frosty Anderson. Rodgers accounted for 30 of Nebraska's points in a 40–6 triumph.

Perhaps the bravest performance in Orange Bowl history belongs to Georgia's Frank Sinkwich, who threw for three touchdowns and ran 44 yards for another in spite of playing with a broken jaw in his team's 40–26 conquest of Texas Christian in 1942. Georgia Tech's Jim Still and Nebraska's Bob Churchich tied Sinkwich's record with three TD tosses,

Still against Kansas in 1948 and Churchich against Alabama in 1966.

A 96-yard TD return of an intercepted lateral by Navy's Greg Mather against Missouri in 1961 and David Baker's 94-yard scoring runback of an interception in Oklahoma's 48–21 victory over Duke in 1958 rank as the most memorable scoring plays by a defender in Orange Bowl history.

Also in that 1958 game, Baker and teammate Brewster Hobby became the first players in Orange

Nebraska's Johnny Rodgers (22) scored four times against Notre Dame in the 1973 Orange Bowl.

Bowl history to catch and throw TD passes in the same game (Rodgers matched the record in 1973). During Oklahoma's 21–6 win over Syracuse in 1959, Hobby connected on the longest TD pass in the Orange Bowl—a 79-yarder to Ross Coyle.

The most touchdowns scored in an Orange Bowl are the nine that Alabama and Syracuse totaled in 1953. A back-up 'Bama quarterback named Bart Starr threw the 22-yard TD pass that gave the Tide a scoring record in a 61–6 triumph.

Four players have made two TD receptions in a single Orange Bowl game—Texas Christian's Bud Alford against Georgia in 1942, Georgia Tech's James Patton against Kansas in 1948, and Alabama's Ray Perkins and Nebraska's Tony Jeter in the same game in 1966.

ORANGE BOWL RESULTS

1935	Bucknell 26, Miami (Fla.) 0
1936	Catholic 20, Mississippi 19
1937	Duquesne 13, Mississippi State 12
1938	Auburn 6, Michigan State 0
1939	Tennessee 17, Oklahoma 0
1940	Georgia Tech 21, Missouri 7
1941	Mississippi State 14, Georgetown 7
1942	Georgia 40, Texas Christian 26
1943	Alabama 37, Boston College 21
1944	Louisiana State 19, Texas A&M 14
1945	Tulsa 26, Georgia Tech 12
1946	Miami (Fla.) 13, Holy Cross 6
1947	Rice 8, Tennessee 0
1948	Georgia Tech 20, Kansas 14

1949 Texas 41, Georgia 28
1950 Santa Clara 21, Kentucky 13
1951 Clemson 15, Miami (Fla.) 14
1952 Georgia Tech 17, Baylor 14
1953 Alabama 61, Syracuse 6
1954 Oklahoma 7, Maryland 0
1955 Duke 34, Nebraska 7
1956 Oklahoma 20, Maryland 6
1957 Colorado 27, Clemson 21
1958 Oklahoma 48, Duke 21
1959 Oklahoma 21, Syracuse 6
1960 Georgia 14, Missouri 0
1961 Missouri 21, Navy 14
1962 Louisiana State 25, Colorado 7
1963 Alabama 17, Oklahoma 0
1964 Nebraska 13, Auburn 7
1965 Texas 21, Alabama 17
1966 Alabama 39, Nebraska 28
1967 Florida 27, Georgia Tech 12
1968 Oklahoma 26, Tennessee 24
1969 Penn State 15, Kansas 14
1970 Penn State 10, Missouri 3
1971 Nebraska 17, Louisiana State 12
1972 Nebraska 38, Alabama 6
1973 Nebraska 40, Notre Dame 6
1974 Penn State 16, Louisiana State 9
1975 Notre Dame 13, Alabama 11
1976 Oklahoma 14, Michigan 6
1977 Ohio State 27, Colorado 10
1978 Arkansas 31, Oklahoma 6
1979 Oklahoma 31, Nebraska 24
1980 Oklahoma 24, Florida State 7
1981 Oklahoma 18, Florida State 17
1982 Clemson 22, Nebraska 15

Appendix

NFL TOUCHDOWN RECORDS

Most Seasons Leading League in TD's
8 Don Hutson, Green Bay, 1935–38, 1941–44

Most TD's
Career: 126 Jimmy Brown, Cleveland, 1957–65
Season: 23 O.J. Simpson, Buffalo, 1975
Rookie Season: 22 Gale Sayers, Chicago, 1965
Game: 6 Ernie Nevers, Chicago Cardinals, vs. Chicago Bears, Nov. 28, 1929; Dub Jones, Cleveland, vs. Chicago Bears, Nov. 25, 1951; Gale Sayers, Chicago, vs. San Francisco, Dec. 12, 1965

Most Games in a Row Scoring TD's
18 Lenny Moore, Baltimore, 1963–65

Most TD's Rushing
Career: 106 Jimmy Brown, Cleveland, 1957–65
Season: 19 Jim Taylor, Green Bay, 1962; Earl Campbell, Houston, 1979; Chuck Muncie, San Diego, 1981
Game: 6 Ernie Nevers, Chicago Cardinals, vs. Chicago Bears, Nov. 28, 1929

Source: *National Football League Record Manual*

Most Games in a Row Rushing for TD's
11 Lenny Moore, Baltimore, 1963–64

Most TD Passes
Career: 342 Fran Tarkenton, Minnesota and N.Y. Giants, 1961–78
Season: 36 George Blanda, Houston, 1961; Y.A. Tittle, N.Y. Giants, 1963
Game: 7 Five players, most recently Joe Kapp, Minnesota, vs. Baltimore, Sept. 28, 1969

Most Games in a Row Passing for TD's
47 Johnny Unitas, Baltimore, 1956–60

Most TD Receptions
Career: 99 Don Hutson, Green Bay, 1935–45
Season: 17 Don Hutson, Green Bay, 1942; Elroy Hirsch, Los Angeles, 1951; Bill Groman, Houston, 1961
Game: 5 Bob Shaw, Chicago Cardinals, vs. Baltimore, Oct. 2, 1950; Kellen Winslow, San Diego, vs. Oakland, Nov. 22, 1981

Most Games in a Row, TD Receptions
11 Elroy Hirsch, Los Angeles, 1950–51; Buddy Dial, Pittsburgh, 1959–60

Most TD's on Interception Returns
Career: 9 Ken Houston, Houston and Washington, 1967–80
Season: 4 Ken Houston, Houston, 1971; Jim Kearney, Kansas City, 1972
Game: 2 Eleven players, most recently Prentice McCray, New England, vs. N.Y. Jets, Nov. 21, 1976

Longest Return of Interception for TD
102 Four players, most recently Louis Breeden, Cincinnati, vs. San Diego, Nov. 8, 1981

Most Punts Returned for TD's
Career: 8 Jack Christiansen, Detroit, 1951–58
Season: 4 Jack Christiansen, Detroit, 1951; Rick Upchurch, Denver, 1976

Game: 2 Three players, most recently Rick Upchurch, Denver, vs. Cleveland, Sept. 26, 1976

Longest Return of Punt for TD

98 Gil LeFebvre, Cincinnati, vs. Brooklyn, Dec. 3, 1933; Charlie West, Minnesota, vs. Washington, Nov. 3, 1968

Most Kickoffs Returned for TD's

Career: 6 Ollie Matson, Chicago Cardinals, Los Angeles, Detroit, Philadelphia, 1952–64; Gale Sayers, Chicago, 1965–71; Travis Williams, Green Bay and Los Angeles, 1967–71

Season: 4 Travis Williams, Green Bay, 1967; Cecil Turner, Chicago, 1970

Game: 2 Timmy Brown, Philadelphia, vs. Dallas, Nov. 6, 1966; Travis Williams, Green Bay, vs. Cleveland, Nov. 12, 1967

Longest Return of Kickoff for TD

106 Al Carmichael, Green Bay, vs. Chicago Bears, Oct. 7, 1956; Noland Smith, Kansas City, vs. Denver, Dec. 17, 1967; Roy Green, St. Louis, vs. Dallas, Oct. 21, 1979

Longest Return of Fumble for TD

104 Jack Tatum, Oakland, vs. Green Bay, Sept. 24, 1972

Longest Return of Missed Field Goal for TD

101 Al Nelson, Philadelphia, vs. Dallas, Sept. 26, 1971

SUPER BOWL TOUCHDOWN RECORDS

Most TD's

Career: 4 Franco Harris, Pittsburgh, four games

Game: 2 Nine players, most recently Chris Ross, Cincinnati, vs. San Francisco, 1982

Source: *National Football League Record Manual*

Most TD's Rushing

Career: 4 Franco Harris, Pittsburgh, four games

Game: 2 Elijah Pitts, Green Bay, vs. Kansas City, 1967; Larry Csonka, Miami, vs. Minnesota, 1974; Pete Banaszak, Oakland, vs. Minnesota, 1977; Franco Harris, Pittsburgh, vs. Los Angeles, 1980

Most TD Passes

Career: 9 Terry Bradshaw, Pittsburgh, four games

Game: 4 Terry Bradshaw, Pittsburgh, vs. Dallas, 1979

Most TD Receptions

Career: 3 John Stallworth, Pittsburgh, and Lynn Swann, Pittsburgh, four games each

Game: 2 Max McGee, Green Bay, vs. Kansas City, 1967; Bill Miller, Oakland, vs. Green Bay, 1968; John Stallworth, Pittsburgh, vs. Dallas, 1979; Cliff Branch, Oakland, vs. Philadelphia, 1981; Chris Ross, Cincinnati, vs. San Francisco, 1982

Most TD's on Interception Returns

Game: 1 Herb Adderley, Green Bay, vs. Oakland, 1968; Willie Brown, Oakland, vs. Minnesota, 1977

Most Fumbles Returned for TD's

Game: 1 Mike Bass, Washington, vs. Miami, 1973; Mike Hegman, Dallas, vs. Pittsburgh, 1979.

SUPER BOWL RESULTS

I, 1967	Green Bay (NFL) 35, Kansas City (AFL) 10
II, 1968	Green Bay (NFL) 33, Oakland (AFL) 14
III, 1969	New York Jets (AFL) 16, Baltimore (NFL) 7
IV, 1970	Kansas City (AFL) 23, Minnesota (NFL) 7
V, 1971	Baltimore (AFC) 16, Dallas (NFC) 13
VI, 1972	Dallas (NFC) 24, Miami (AFC) 3
VII, 1973	Miami (AFC) 14, Washington (NFC) 7
VIII, 1974	Miami (AFC) 24, Minnesota (NFC) 7

IX, 1975	Pittsburgh (AFC) 16, Minnesota (NFC) 6
X, 1976	Pittsburgh (AFC) 21, Dallas (NFC) 17
XI, 1977	Oakland (AFC) 32, Minnesota (NFC) 14
XII, 1978	Dallas (NFC) 27, Denver (AFC) 10
XIII, 1979	Pittsburgh (AFC) 35, Dallas (NFC) 31
XIV, 1980	Pittsburgh (AFC) 31, Los Angeles (NFC) 19
XV, 1981	Oakland (AFC) 27, Philadelphia (NFC) 10
XVI, 1982	San Francisco (NFC) 26, Cincinnati (AFC) 21

NCAA MAJOR COLLEGE (DIVISION I) TOUCHDOWN RECORDS

Responsible for Most TD's

Career: 120 Neil Lomax, Portland State, 1977–80 (scored 14, passed for 106)

Season: 53 Jim McMahon, Brigham Young, 1980 (scored 6, passed for 47)

Game: 9 Dennis Shaw, San Diego State, vs. New Mexico State, Nov. 15, 1969 (passed for 9); Jerry Rhome, Tulsa, vs. Louisville, Oct. 17, 1964 (scored 2, passed for 7); Neil Lomax, Portland State, vs. Delaware State, Nov. 8, 1980 (scored 1, passed for 8)

Most TD's

Career: 59 Tony Dorsett, Pittsburgh, 1973–76; Glenn Davis, Army, 1943–46

3-Year Career: 56 Steve Owens, Oklahoma, 1967–69

Season: 29 Lydell Mitchell, Penn State, 1971

Game: 7 Arnold Boykin, Mississippi, vs. Mississippi State, Dec. 1, 1951

Most TD's Rushing

Career: 56 Steve Owens, Oklahoma, 1967–69

Source: *NCAA Football Records*

Season: 26 Lydell Mitchell, Penn State, 1971
Game: 7 Arnold Boykin, Mississippi, vs. Mississippi State, Dec. 1, 1951

Most TD's Rushing by a Freshman
Season: 15 Herschel Walker, Georgia, 1980
Game: 5 Mike Northington, Purdue, vs. Iowa, Nov. 3, 1973

Most TD Passes
Career: 84 Jim McMahon, Brigham Young, 1977–80
Season: 47 Jim McMahon, Brigham Young, 1980
Game: 9 Dennis Shaw, San Diego State, vs. New Mexico State, Nov. 15, 1969
Half: 7 Neil Lomax, Portland State, vs. Delaware State, Nov. 8, 1980 (first); Dennis Shaw, San Diego State, vs. New Mexico State, Nov. 15, 1969 (first)
Quarter: 7 Neil Lomax, Portland State, vs. Delaware State, Nov. 8, 1980 (first)

Most Games in a Row Passing for TD's
Career: 18 Steve Ramsey, North Texas State (Oct. 5, 1968, through Nov. 22, 1969)

Most TD Passes First Game of a Career
5 John Reaves, Florida, vs. Houston, Sept. 20, 1969

Most TD Passes by a Freshman
Season: 18 Mark Herrmann, Purdue, 1977
Game: 6 Bob Hoernschemeyer, Indiana, vs. Nebraska, Oct. 9, 1943

Most TD Receptions
Career: 34 Elmo Wright, Houston, 1968–70
Season: 18 Tom Reynolds, San Diego State, 1969
Game: 6 Tim Delaney, San Diego State, vs. New Mexico State, Nov. 15, 1969

Most TD Receptions by a Freshman
Season: 10 Dwight Collins, Pittsburgh, 1980

Most TD's on Interception Returns

Career: 5 Jackie Walker, Tennessee, 1969–71

Season: 3 Eleven players, last done by Ken Thomas, San Jose State, 1979

Game: 2 Many players, last done by Brian Baggott, UCLA, vs. California, October 21, 1978

Most TD's on Punt Returns

Career: 7 Johnny Rodgers, Nebraska, 1970–72; Jack Mitchell, Oklahoma, 1946–48

Game: 2 Many players, last done by Robert Woods, Grambling, vs. Southern, Nov. 26, 1977

Most TD's on Kickoff Returns

Career: 6 Anthony Davis, USC, 1972–74

Season: 3 Willie Gault, Tennessee, 1980; Anthony Davis, USC, 1974; Stan Brown, Purdue, 1970; Forrest Hall, San Francisco, 1946

Game: 2 Anthony Davis, USC, vs. Notre Dame, Dec. 2, 1972; Ollie Matson, San Francisco, vs. Fordham, Oct. 20, 1951; Ron Horwath, Detroit, vs. Hillsdale, Sept. 22, 1950; Paul Copolous, Marquette, vs. Iowa Pre-Flight, Nov. 6, 1943

Most Games in a Row Scoring a TD

Career: 23 Bill Burnett, Arkansas (Oct. 5, 1968, through Oct. 21, 1970)